SOMATIC
PSYCHOTHERAPY
TOOLBOX

125 Worksheets & Exercises
to Treat Trauma & Stress

Manuela Mischke-Reeds, MA, LMFT

PRAISE FOR SOMATIC PSYCHOTHERAPY TOOLBOX

"A thorough, thoughtful, and immensely practical workbook written to help therapists work with clients' bodily responses, not just with their actions and emotions. Manuela Mischke-Reeds has a compassionate voice that imbues her very precise somatic interventions and suggestions with warmth and clinical wisdom."

-Janina Fisher, PhD
World Renowned Trauma Expert and Author

"Manuela brings to this intricate and useful guidebook a lifetime of working skillfully on the edges between life journeys and the challenges posed by our being flesh. While there have been so many positive turns towards the significance of our embodiment in recent decades, much remains on the surface, brought to light by such simple principles as noticing our breathing and our feet on the ground. But there is so much more to discover in the depths. More profound and risky journeys require an experienced guide to navigate safely the intricacies of the vast wilds of our bodies to uncover the beauty, wisdom and healing potentials that lie beyond our ordinary awareness. This book gives so many helpful avenues for exploration into unexpected revelations."

-Don Hanlon Johnson, PhD
Founder of the Somatics Psychology Graduate Program,
California Institute of Integral Studies

Somatic Psychotherapy Toolbox © 2018 by Manuela Mischke-Reeds

Published by
PESI Publishing & Media
PESI, Inc
3839 White Ave
Eau Claire, WI 54703

Editing: Donald Altman & Michelle Nelson
Layout: Bookmasters & Amy Rubenzer
Cover: Amy Rubenzer

ISBN: 9781683731351

Proudly printed in the United States.

PESI
Publishing
& Media
www.publishing.pesi.com

Be kind to your body — your inseparable best friend.

"Our body is a source of truth."

-Albert Pesso

"If you're an alive body, no one can tell you how to experience the world.
And no one can tell you what the truth is, because you experience it for yourself."

-Stanley Keleman

"The human body is not an instrument to be used, but a realm of one's being
to be experienced, explored, enriched and thereby educated."

-Thomas Hanna

"The body is your nearest environment."

-Jean Klein

Table of Contents

Acknowledgments xv

About the Author xvii

Chapter 1: INTRODUCTION 3
    Why Every Therapist Needs to Integrate the Body in Psychotherapy
    What is Different About This Book?
    Four Signposts on Your Journey

Section 1: GUIDELINES - DEFINING AND WORKING WITH THE BODY

Chapter 2: WHAT IS SOMA? 9

Chapter 3: WHAT TO LOOK OUT FOR 13

Chapter 4: GUIDELINES AND SAFETY 15

Section 2: THE THERAPIST'S TOOLKIT

Chapter 5: SELF-SKILLS: PREPARED AND GROUNDED 21

Preparation - Somatic Awareness in Your Own Body
    Tool #1: Taking a Body Snapshot for the Day
    Tool #2: Back-Body Awareness for Therapy Readiness
    Tool #3: Grounding Through the Body
    Tool #4: Shaking It Off (Laying Down)
    Tool #5: Calling the Internal Support Team
    Tool #6: Self-Resourcing - Floor Work
    Tool #7: Somatic Inventory of Burnout Signs

Chapter 6: THERAPEUTIC ATTITUDE WHEN WORKING WITH THE BODY 35

Embracing an Experiential View
    Tool #8: Open Attention Technique
    Tool #9: Focused Attention
    Tool #10: Moving Between Open and Focused Attention

Chapter 7: HOW TO FACILITATE THE SOMATIC PROCESS. 43

The Question We Never Ask
   Tool #11: "Let's Experiment! Would You Like to Try Something?"
   Tool #12: Making Empathic Statements
   Tool #13: Asking the Right Questions
   Tool #14: Guiding into the Soma
   Tool #15: What Else?
   Tool #16: Listening to the Body

Chapter 8: TRACKING TOOLS 55

What and How to Track the Body
   Tool #17: 5 Kinds of Tracking
   Tool #18: Tracking the Body Checklist
   Tool #19: Tracking for Trauma Cues
   Tool #20: Tracking My Body Chart

Section 3: INTEGRATING SOMATIC THERAPY TOOLS IN PRACTICE

Chapter 9: MINDFULNESS AND BODY. 69

What is Embodied Mindfulness?
Pitfalls When Working with Mindfulness
Remedy the Pitfalls
   Tool #21: How to Induce Mindfulness
   Tool #22: Cultivating Self - Witnessing-Suspend the Moment
   Tool #23: Befriending the Body
   Tool #24: Relaxing Rest
   Tool #25: Moving Body Scan
   Tool #26: Walking Meditation
   Tool #27: Simple Earth Mindfulness

Chapter 10: BODY AWARENESS AND BODY READING 83
   Tool #28: Global Awareness of Body
   Tool #29: Body Awareness Inventory
   Tool #30: Naming Your Present-Moment Experience in Your Body
   Tool #31: Identifying Body Themes
   Tool #32: Somatic Beliefs of Self
   Tool #33: Mapping the Body
   Tool #34: Body Reading for the Therapist

Chapter 11: THE SOMAGRAM AND BODY PARTS. 95
   Tool #35: Somagram #1
   Tool #36: Somagram #2 - Free Charting

Working with Body Splits
   Tool #37: Left/Right Body Split
   Tool #38: Upper/Lower Body Split
   Tool #39: Front/Back Body Split
   Tool #40: Body Splits

Chapter 12: PRESENCE, PERCEPTION AND SENSATIONS 105

Tool #41: Soft Vision
Tool #42: Gentle Head Lift
Tool #43: Hands Over Eye Sockets
Tool #44: Sensing Your Fluid Brain
Tool #45: The Spaces In-Between
Tool #46: Dual Awareness
Tool #47: Bumper Stickers - Reminders for the Body
Tool #48: Sensing Space

Chapter 13: MOVEMENT INTERVENTIONS 115

Movement Takes All Forms
Tool #49: Unfurling
Tool #50: Wet Sandbag
Tool #51: Micro-Movement in Neck
Tool #52: Opening the Horizon
Tool #53: Walking with Aim
Tool #54: Mirror, Mirror
Tool #55: Movement Play and Beliefs
Tool #56: Figure 8 Resource Movement
Tool #57: Defending Arms
Tool #58: Orienting Movements

Chapter 14: BOUNDARIES 131

The Importance of Setting Boundaries
Tool #59: Body Boundary
Tool #60: Extending a Physical Boundary
Tool #61: Muscle Tone Boundary
Tool #62: Wrapping Yourself into Your Own Space
Tool #63: Personal Space Exploration
Tool #64: Boundary Homework for Personal Space
Tool #65: When Boundary is Violated - Re-drawing the Territory
Tool #66: Personal Space in Relation
Tool #67: String Exercise in Relationship

Chapter 15: POSTURE 147

Posture and Internal Messages
Tool #68: The Lengthy Spine
Tool #69: Grounding Through the Spine
Tool #70: Inner Alignment
Tool #71: Somatic Strength Posture
Tool #72: Posture Snapshot
Tool #73: Draw Your Skeleton

Chapter 16: GESTURE AND NON-VERBAL COMMUNICATION 157

Non-Verbal Communication
    Tool #74: Non-Verbal Communications Chart
    Tool #75: Tracking the Meaning of Gestures
    Tool #76: Centered Hands
    Tool #77: Midline Gestures

Chapter 17: EMOTIONS AND SELF-REGULATION 165

Soma, Emotions and the Art of Self-Regulation
    Tool #78: Meaning Making: High-Road vs. Low-Road
    Tool #79: Emotions Chart - Self-Assessment and Emotional Themes
    Tool #80: Lean Back to Lean In
    Tool #81: Managing the "Too Much"
    Tool #82: Sailing the Midline
    Tool #83: Sitting Run

Chapter 18: BODY AND SELF-IMAGE 173

    Tool #84: Body Image – Inside-Out vs. Outside-In
    Tool #85: Shifting the Perception
    Tool #86: Body Drawing
    Tool #87: Breathing into the Seven Energy Centers

Chapter 19: BREATH AWARENESS AND TECHNIQUES 183

Guidelines When Working with Breath
The Truth About Deep Breathing
How to Use the Breathing Tools
    Tool #88: Round-Wave Breath
    Tool #89: Breathing Towards Calm - Regulate Your Breath
    Tool #90: Lateral Breathing Sequence
    Tool #91: Three-Part Breathing Sequence
    Tool #92: Cellular Breathing
    Tool #93: Deflating the Tire of Anxiety
    Tool #94: Lunar Breath - Diffusing the Tension

Chapter 20: WORKING WITH SOUND AND VOICE 195

    Tool #95: Listening Bell
    Tool #96: Sounding into the Body
    Tool #97: "Hmmm" Sound
    Tool #98: Corridor of Sound

Chapter 21: WORKING WITH SAFE TOUCH 201

Why is Touch Important?
General Therapeutic Guidelines
When to Potentially Use Safe Touch
Tips for Using Touch
    Tool #99: Self-Touch - Tapping
    Tool #100: Cueing Hands
    Tool #101: Compassionate Self-Touch

Section 4: SOMATIC TOOLS FOR STRESS AND TRAUMA

Chapter 22: TRAUMA AND THE BODY 209

Polyvagal Theory: A Very Brief Overview
    Tool #102: Tracking Your Own Nervous System
    Tool #103: Expanded Window of Tolerance Chart
    Tool #104: How Can I Resource Myself?
    Tool #105: Scanning Towards Safety
    Tool #106: MOVE!
    Tool #107: Imagine Running Faster Than the Tiger
    Tool #108: The Container Principle
    Tool #109: Tracking Triggers Chart
    Tool #110: Trauma Stressor Timeline
    Tool #111: Shaking to Safety
    Tool #112: Orienting Gong Awareness
    Tool #113: Calling Your Experience by Its True Name
    Tool #114: Releasing the Psoas Muscle

Chapter 23: SOMATIC RESOURCING 235

Somatic Resources - Thriving Resources
Cultivating Dual Awareness
    Tool #115: Five-Step Resourcing
    Tool #116: Dual Awareness Practice
    Tool #117: Flat Back Strength
    Tool #118: Embodied Self-Awareness and Resourcing
    Tool #119: Name Your Resource
Somatic Coherence
    Tool #120: Reflect on Your Own Somatic Coherence
    Tool #121: Tracking Your Client from Body Activation to Somatic Coherence

Chapter 24: SHAME AND TRAUMA 251

Shame and Somatic Interventions
Verbal Cues
Breathing Cues
    Tool #122: Intervention Sequence with Shame
    Tool #123: Outing the Shame Monster
    Tool #124: Part 1: Identifying and Reframing Shame Attacks
        Part 2: Identifying Shame Attacks and Preventing Shame Spirals
    Tool #125: Sun Rays into Your Body

Bibliography 261

Acknowledgments

Somatic Psychotherapy has a long and intertwined tradition of various somatic schools and thought. The techniques listed in this book can be found in many different somatic schools. I have used many of these techniques over my 25 years of clinical practice and they have changed and shifted with my clients' input over the years. It is through the results of the client's healing that we can see the true transformational power of somatic work.

I want to acknowledge some of the notable influences that have shaped my professional life and teaching. I want to recognize the influences of Hakomi Psychotherapy and the talented Hakomi trainers around the globe that I have had the privilege of working alongside. A special thank you to Somatic Experiencing and Dr. Peter Levine, Dr. Marianna Eckberg, and Sensorymotor Founder Dr. Pat Odgen, all who inspired me into my early career path as a trauma therapist. I also want to recognize Continuum Movement founders, Emilie Conrad and Susan Harper. The influences of Gestalt Therapy, Hanna Somatics, Bodynamics, Janina Fisher, Don Johnson, Ann Halprin, and Babette Rothschild's trauma work, EMDR, can also be found in this book. In addition, I acknowledge the influence of Reggie Ray for inspiring me to experience meditation practice as embodiment of spiritual practice.

About the Author

Manuela Mischke-Reeds, MA, LMFT, is a licensed somatic psychotherapist, international teacher and speaker, author and Meditation teacher. She trains health professionals in California, Australia, New Zealand, Israel, Europe and China. Additionally, she co-directs and teaches at the Hakomi Institute of California; and she is the developer of "From Trauma to Dharma," a somatic trauma training for health professionals.

Manuela lectures, consults and trains professionals in the health sector and in corporate settings on stress, trauma, mindfulness and well-being. Her work focuses on how to live from an embodied and mindful knowing in our own bodies. Understanding the intelligence of our own bodies is key to accessing and sustaining mental health and well-being. She believes that every person can access their own inherent body health and wisdom despite any emotional stressors or traumas of the past. She works and practices in Menlo Park, CA.

Manuela has published *8 Keys to Practicing Mindfulness: Practical Strategies for Emotional Health and Well-Being* (W.W. Norton, 2015), and was also a contributor to *Hakomi Mindfulness-Centered Somatic Psychotherapy* (W.W. Norton, 2015). She also contributed to *The Praeger Handbook of Community Mental Health Practice* (Praeger, 2013).

www.manuelamischkereeds.com

INTRODUCTION

CHAPTER 1
Introduction

WHY EVERY THERAPIST NEEDS TO INTEGRATE THE BODY IN PSYCHOTHERAPY

We think we live in our bodies. But how do many of us really inhabit full-body awareness? Mental health clinicians know that trauma, stress, anxiety and depression can catapult clients into a myriad of symptoms, including insomnia, irritability, emotional dysregulation, anxiety, panic attacks, depressed body feelings, and more. It's easy to think that these symptoms can be healed by working with thought patterns and emotions alone. The truth is that we live and dream in the body. Symptoms are of the body. Yet, we rarely consider the body as the source and inspiration for healing. We perceive the world around us through our body responses. Not sleeping well, ruminating thoughts, worries about family or the future, grief and trauma have devastating health effects. The body is under attack, and we can't heal the body with the mind alone.

During my 25 years in clinical practice, many clients have courageously shared their body stories with me. Often they described experiencing a profound disconnect from themselves, feeling out of touch or worse: "being out of my body." When we as humans are out of touch with our bodies we are out of touch with life. Habits can mask pain, and anxiety can give way to habits and addiction. The deep desire to be fully embodied exists in everyone. In my years of listening to many clients and students one thing is clear: We want to be alive in our bodies, living fully in our experience. And yet, the natural wisdom towards the body is not well practiced in the clinical room.

Whatever clinical modality we practice as clinicians, we are all sitting in front of a breathing and dynamic body. This book is designed to help therapists incorporate all different kinds of somatic awareness. For example, there are patterns of breath, skin changes, eye movements, posture, and subtle movements and gestures that all express moods, feelings and inner landscapes that we can learn to study and effectively work with. Enhancing a client's body awareness is a powerful tool for transformation. Of course, this work is not just for the patient or client. The therapist who calmly sits within themselves can learn to somatically reference their own body state. This, in turn, sets the stage to facilitate the somatic discovery of a client's inner world and body wisdom.

Another approach that will be utilized in these pages is that of mindfulness. Mindfulness has made a big impact in our society and psychological field these past years. Many clinicians have incorporated mindfulness into their modalities. When mindfulness is used, the client is referencing their somatic awareness, how they "feel" inside. But often there is lack of follow-up on how to facilitate the somatic feelings into a coherent experience. In short, clients learn to get mindful, but not how to journey into the somatic experience safely. This is critical when working with trauma and stress.

Many therapists ask me HOW they should facilitate these body feelings and basic body awareness. How can I get my client to be more embodied? What do I do? Can you suggest any ideas I can offer to my client somatically? These are some of the questions my colleagues and students have asked me over the years. Because every therapist needs to have a basic somatic repertoire, those questions are answered in *Somatic Psychotherapy Toolbox: 125 Worksheets and Exercises to Treat Trauma & Stress*.

Our collective psychotherapy field has matured to the point where we can afford to cross pollinate and learn from various therapy disciplines so we can benefit our clients. It is in this spirit that I offer these potent somatic techniques for you to use with your clients. Working with the somatic experience of the client should be as natural as any psychological tool we use. We are sitting with the greatest asset of healing and well-being: the client's innate body wisdom.

WHAT IS DIFFERENT ABOUT THIS BOOK?

The Cartesian split of the body-mind is alive and well in our dominant culture. We "think" that we can overcome problems with cognitive reasoning alone. Western psychology has a bias towards mind over body, rather than a trust of the body's intelligence. Feelings and sensations have been marginalized when connected with body awareness. This may play a role in why somatic techniques have not yet been widely integrated into mainstream psychotherapy. Yet, the holistic awareness of body-mind is critical in any healing of mental ailments and physical challenges our clients face.

Deep cultural beliefs impact how we view the body. When working with the body, we need to respect and learn about these cultural imprints as part of understanding our own, and the client's, biases. The recognition that emotions are intelligent opens the first door that healing is more than thinking. The decade of the brain has brought the awareness to how thinking patterns influence the body. The recognition is now that our experiences are interconnected with our brain states, emotional patterns, what we believe, and how we inhabit our bodies.

The mindfulness wave has brought us tools to inquire, calm the busy mind, and listen to the undercurrents of our heart. It also has highlighted the global need for stress relief, the value for quiet and the pathway to self-actualization and health. We also have discovered the power of now. The only time in the past-present-future continuum we can actually create change is in the now. We now need to integrate the decade of the brain and the discovery of mindfulness into our lived experience of the body. Somatic techniques can bridge the discoveries of brain and mind into how we inquire into our live experience. To be fully embodied is a journey each human can make.

Trauma truncates the client away from the body, their healthy mind and heart, and corrupts the awareness of the body. One of the reasons that somatic techniques have been so successful with trauma clients is that the trauma client sees how far they have gotten away from their innate health. In each trauma client I have met there is both a dread of trauma symptoms and a deep desire to come back to a holistic sense of self. This desire is a deep knowing from the body that there is a pathway back to health. That sense is somatic awareness.

This book aims to teach the client and therapist tools to aid the journey back to the body, health, and wisdom.

It is important to note that the sensitivity of the therapist is critical. The therapist can't successfully facilitate somatic work without having done it themselves. The embodied therapist will know how to guide the client back to their body wisdom. The therapist toolkit needs to be eclectic enough to offer somatic techniques that fit the client in the moment. Being in one's own body wisdom will attune you to be open and receptive for what is right to offer to the client. That is when true and lasting transformation can occur.

FOUR SIGNPOSTS ON YOUR JOURNEY

This book has four distinct sections. **Section 1** prepares the clinician to think about basic guidelines and understand the importance of working with the body. Here you observe how to safely set up somatic interventions. The key to success is incorporating these exciting techniques into your existing clinical repertoire. The clinician's keen eye to detail and what I call "tracking," or noticing the subtle changes, makes all the difference when offering a nuanced intervention that is truly beneficial for the client. Please spend some time reading the basic guidelines and safety aspects in Chapter 4 to set yourself up for the right mindset—one that is open and receptive.

Section 2 addresses the various and concrete tools you can use to prepare for working somatically with clients. This is a critical part of working somatically—the therapist's own cultivation of their somatic wisdom and readiness. This section includes tools and methods for you to use and become familiar with.

Section 3 looks at integrating the somatic tools into your existing practice. Somatic intervention can be easily combined and integrated into existing modalities you are already comfortable with. Especially if you have an orientation towards mindfulness in your work, these techniques will feel like a natural extension of what you have been doing. Mindfulness and the use of mindfulness from a body-oriented perspective are key to the successful implementation of these techniques. The client and therapist need to have a perceptive eye towards the changes of the body. There is a range of techniques and ways of working, from using the medium of body drawing, to safe movement interventions that are applicable to a wide audience, to physicalizing boundaries and posture. These tools will aid the therapist in deepening the client's healing into themselves.

Body and breath awareness are the heart of any somatic technique. There is a section that highlights these techniques and offers concrete steps to working with them. I also include the use of safe touch, which each therapist will need to use their own discretion on based on the benefits, their licensure and comfort level, and the comfort level of the client. To not include the use of touch would be a gross violation of what somatic techniques stand for, yet we need to use the standard of care in applying such interventions. Please familiarize yourself with the standard of care in your state and licensure. (For example, in the state of California, there is great caution amongst licensed psychotherapists in the use of touch.) There are many ethical considerations in how to use it safely and appropriately, yet it is legal to use touch. Please consider the law and ethics of your state before using safe touch.

Section 4 looks more in-depth at the targeted somatic interventions that are helpful with trauma and stress clients. A high percentage of PTSD and stress disorder clients suffer from somatic complaints and the inclusion of the body is a big factor in trauma memory recovery and the healing of trauma symptoms. I highlight the importance of somatically resourcing the client and techniques to aid this, as this is a central tenet of the somatic trauma work.

Exercises and Worksheets

 Therapist Exercises and Worksheets are meant for use by the therapist themselves.

 Client Exercises are to be used with the client in-session or as homework.

 Client Worksheets can be given to clients to complete.

SECTION 1
GUIDELINES - Defining and Working with the Body

CHAPTER 2
What is Soma?

"Somatic awareness is at the cutting edge….and represents a way to truly empower individuals in their efforts to maintain or restore good health. Somatic awareness constitutes an innate wisdom that people have about their own psychobiological health…Somatic awareness represents the next state of evolution of holistic care."

- Donald Bakal

WHAT IS THE SOMA?

The Greek *soma* means the body. *Psyche* means mind. Therefore, Somatic Psychotherapy is the study of the body-mind interface. Referring to the soma in the context of psychotherapy is to reference the ability to sense oneself through sensations. Interoception is the capacity to feel one's present body through emotions, sensations and different body states. Feelings and emotions are often understood as interchangeable. They are interconnected, but distinct. Emotions are lower level and sensory-based responses such as biochemical changes of the brain. Feelings begin in the neo-cortical regions of the brain and are important for our memory consolidation. Emotions begin before our feelings. Emotions are primal, direct and physical. Dr. Antonio Damasio calls feelings "mental experiences of body states which arise as the brain interprets emotions." Throughout the book I will use the word "feeling" with clients for their ease of understanding. I often use the word "experience" as this will be more precise in eliciting the emotions and the somatic experience we are after in this book. This will help you to look for the more primal experiences from the soma. Sensations can be experienced on their own and can provide a direct experience of one's body that can deliver new information to the self. For example, you can be eating ice cream and enjoy the chocolate hazelnut flavor without the emotions. Yet, you can also have the thought of eating this same ice cream on your recent vacation to Florence, which will flood you with sensations, as well as emotions and memories. This coupling of emotions-sensations-memories is often what we encounter when clients get stuck in traumatic memory or haunting images.

The other ability is the proprioceptive sense. This self-awareness is experienced through the movement of the body. We discover where we are in time and space through our proprioception. The interplay of interoception and proprioception through the nerve and spinal pathways of body and brain integrate into one cohesive awareness of the body. This integration is felt through emotions and sensations.

DEFINING SOMATIC PSYCHOTHERAPY

Somatic psychotherapy is an integrative approach to treating the whole human being. A person's thoughts, feelings, sensations, attitude and belief systems all have an impact on the physical well-being of that person. How is the person experiencing themselves in the various categories of their existence? What do they believe about themselves? And where are these beliefs narrow or limiting to the degree that they impact physical and emotional well-being?

The somatic psychotherapist views the body and mind as essentially interconnected and investigates how the person expresses themselves in posture, gesture, muscular patterns, emotional patterns and physiological arousals; and then helps facilitate self-regulation processes when the body-mind has become imbalanced.

Somatic psychotherapy is highly effective with trauma-associated symptoms because these are often experienced very physically in the body. Somatic psychotherapy uses mindfulness, body awareness, breath awareness and body-oriented tools to guide the client towards their inner and outer resources to stabilize any dysregulated symptomology. Clients can then mindfully explore options for resolving emotional and physiological patterns.

WHY IS EMBODIMENT SO IMPORTANT?

"Embodied self-awareness is the ability to pay attention to ourselves, to feel our sensations, emotions, and movements online, in the present moment, without the mediating influence of judgmental thoughts."

-Allen Fogel

We live in a disembodied culture. We spend more and more time entertaining our boredom and short attention spans with media and information and less time feeling and sensing our responses to what we are consuming. The result is a sense of physical and emotional disconnection ranging from numbing to dissociation and apathy. In short, we lose the connection with embodied self-awareness. Fortunately, embodiment lessens the numbing that occurs.

When we are embodied we feel for others. Through empathy, we resonate with the pain of others and we can become active in protecting the vulnerable, or the environment, around us because we care. Getting disconnected from our sense of embodied self brings us into direct disconnect with our larger body: the Earth. The numbers are clear: Fewer people spend time in nature, more children are glued to their devices and games than ever before, and adults numb out with entertainment, news tidbits and distractions. Whole new social media and news industries are flourishing with this new global addiction, and the result is the disconnection of the body.

Many people don't have a daily, regular practice of coming back to their bodies. We sense and feel through our bodies every minute of the day, yet we seldom become aware that we are doing this. **Only when tensions or pain in the body arise do we pay attention to what is happening.**

Another way to think about this is that embodiment ensures our survival. For instance, when we can't feel pain, we might get hurt: We can't sense the heat on the stove burning our hand. Therefore, pain is a necessary alarm bell from our body alerting us to danger and survival. When we love deeply or take pleasure in a touch, we can feel the expansion and **feelings of safety** that arise with it. We describe this as being more connected or close, at home, or a feeling of warmth. These perceptions of the body are driven by our exteroception (a sensitivity to a stimuli that originates outside of your body) and interoception (a sensitivity to a stimuli originating inside of your body).

Embodiment is feeling oneself directly, without the constant narration or interpretation of our thinking mind. This embodiment has no judgment, no commentary from an inner belief, and no filters, but rather presents the raw data of the body "as is." We can call this present-moment body awareness—direct communication from our deeper self or embodiment. This is a moment in which we are not bound by past or future, and can live in the present moment. We often describe this simple yet elusive sense as coming home, being close to oneself, or simply here.

This points us to the value of being-ness rather than doing-ness. We perhaps would translate this in modern terms of being mindful of one's experience. Although we are currently in the midst of incorporating mindfulness awareness as an acceptable pathway towards health and healing, we are still neglecting the direct communication from the body to ourselves through our soma. The Cartesian spilt we have experienced through the industrial revolution—the disconnection of mind and body, and the value that thoughts are more powerful or to be trusted over what the body communicates—still holds a cultural norm.

"In recent centuries people have not been accustomed to think of their bodies as an active source of meaning."
- Don Johnson

Eugene Gendlin, the founder of Focusing, called this the felt sense describing an intuitive body-feel. This differs from feeling in that one's bodily awareness is experienced as ongoing with the inner and outer perception as a lived experience.

INTEGRATE SOMATIC TECHNIQUES INTO EXISTING PRACTICES

Somatic psychotherapy techniques are **easily integrated into your existing therapy intervention toolbox**. If you already have a mindfulness-based orientation, the bridge to the somatic toolkit is not far.

What is important to note is that you need to inform and include clients in the decision-making when using these techniques. An easy way to do this is to propose an experiment, such as simply asking: "Would you like to try an experiment?" or "How about we try this exercise?"

By asking the client, not only are you showing respect, but you are also setting up a frame of mind that is "experimental," and thus can be successful, can be adjusted, or can be studied and improved upon. Somatic interventions are experiments for the client to help them find out for themselves what works and what doesn't. In this approach, we can empower the client towards their self-advocacy and self-awareness.

Make sure you suggest, explain and then follow up with the results. Explaining ahead what the exercise or practice is makes it safe and accessible for the client. It makes them feel like they are participating rather than being told what to do.

In addition, make sure you are open to suggestions by the client to change something about the exercise; invite collaboration. Make sure that, like a good scientist, you check where you start, suggest the experiments, and then follow up with what has been different. What are the results? Most somatic techniques aim at improving self-awareness and invite the client to discover what THEY can do differently. In my opinion, the most sustainable and long-lasting kind of intervention occurs when the client discovers the change for themselves.

Setting it up right:

1. Suggest the exercise
2. Get their buy-in or permission to try something new
3. Follow through with the instructions
4. Summarize the outcome

Some sample ways to suggest incorporating somatic techniques:

- "Would you like to try this exercise?"
- "How about we try this practice?"
- "Let's find out if we can help you do _____ with this next experience."
- "Are you interested in trying the following exploration?"

BASIC BODY WISDOM PRINCIPLES

The basic body wisdom principles that follow are a reminder of the simple truths of the body's capacities and tendencies. Keep these in mind as you are introducing them and working with your clients. You may even decide to print these out for your client, to give them a fresh perspective on connecting with the body. This can also help them remember that body experiences—whether perceived as positive or negative—are not "set in stone," but of a transient nature. When confronted with chronic pain, clients can lose track of the transient nature of pain and be stuck in the perception that their pain will "last forever." Working with the body means also working with the minds perceptions of the body. Also keep in mind that the brain and body are connected.

Seven Body Wisdom Principles

1. The body responds to external environment with constriction, blockage, muscle tension or unbalance, and acts in unhealthy habits when stressed, physiologically or emotionally threatened, or misused.

2. The body remembers implicitly feelings, sensations and memories when vulnerable, emotional, triggered or touched.

3. The body changes all the time. It's flexible and moldable.

4. The body's experience is transient and does not last. Even pain will subside.

5. The body is capable of repair and healing at any time.

6. The body's wisdom comes forth when attended to, or related to, with kindness, curiosity and patience.

7. The body is the most important place for healing and transformation.

CHAPTER 3
What to Look Out For

UNDERSTANDING BODY SYMPTOMS

The body expresses itself through the landscape of feelings, sensations and tensions. That's why understanding and correctly assessing for body symptoms, or cues, is the key in successfully delivering somatic techniques. For example, you might hear a client say, "I have a tight shoulder because I slept wrong," and brush this off as the truth. But through the somatic lens, you can see this as a cue of the body to be discovered. A simple, "Let's pay attention to that shoulder right now. See what you can sense or feel as you slow down," can bring forth a meaningful and increased level of body awareness.

Learning about your client's individual expression is a very big factor in somatic psychotherapy work. You will want to pay attention to how the body moves, how the client talks about their body, and how they respond in their body when more emotional material surfaces. You want to understand **WHAT** the client is saying in relation to **HOW** they are expressing it in their body. Hearing a client mention places in the body that are painful or experiencing recurring pain can be an indicator that this is something requiring greater attention. You can choose not to pursue it, or you can decide to see if there is something there to be discovered. Learning to carefully observe this unspoken language is what matters.

WHICH CLIENTS CAN BENEFIT FROM SOMATIC INTERVENTIONS?

Although we all can benefit from somatic psychotherapy work, we need to assess and be sensitive to which clients would thrive using somatic interventions, and which clients would not.

Often, clients will voice their discontentment of other approaches they have tried and have had limited success with. Statements such as, *"Talk therapy has been helpful, but has not resolved any of my physical complaints,"* or *"Nothing is changing my patterns, my relationships, or how I am with myself,"* are common. In my own practice, I have typically worked with three types of clients. The first are ones who are informed about somatic work and want to try it; the second are those who are referred because of their "unexplainable" somatic symptoms; and the third are trauma clients who are stuck in their memory resolution or strong trauma symptoms.

Here are some guidelines for working somatically with these three types:

1. The first guideline is to inform the client of somatic interventions and explain what these entail and what they do not. For example, some somatic interventions focus on body movement and can make the client uncomfortable if that is not framed correctly. The use of touch can be a very difficult terrain to navigate, as this can breach into ethical and legal issues. (More on this later in Chapter 21: Working with Safe Touch.)

2. The client needs to agree and be open to working with the body. This is key, as somatic interventions have a component of mindful exploration and experimentation. These interventions need the receptivity of the client to work effectively.

3. Trauma clients are often ideal candidates for somatic psychotherapy, as their symptoms and experience are often "bodily based" and can be helped through it. It is important to assess for the client's readiness and to make sure the client is informed of the approach. No surprises! A trauma survivor needs to know what is happening prior to the exercise so their safety needs are addressed.

4. Unexplainable somatic symptoms are a common referral for somatic psychotherapists. It is important that these somatic complaints are checked out by a medical professional to rule out organic origins before assuming these symptoms are of psychosomatic nature. For example, I had a client who was referred to me with allergy symptoms that could not be explained, and it was assumed that she was "making this up." After careful assessment, and in cooperation with medical professionals, we found a combination to be true. She did have some genuine food allergies, but also had psychosomatic symptoms that were of an emotional nature, as she was distressed about her radical diet, the restriction in her life, and childhood traumas. In such cases, a combination of medical attention and somatic psychotherapy offers the best solution.

5. The informed client is, of course, ideal, but even here it is important not to assume an unconditioned openness to all interventions. As well as offering somatic interventions in the spirit of "trying things out for the client to see, study and learn," it makes sense for you, as a clinician, to study the outcome of your interventions and make adjustments when they are not fruitful.

WHEN NOT TO OFFER SOMATIC INTERVENTIONS

Make sure you assess for somatic readiness in your client. If you encounter fear or resistance, it is better to wait and work in other ways. You can always return to somatic interventions later when there is more safety and interest, or decide not to use them at all. Special attention should be given to clients who have experienced physical and boundary violations of any kind, as well as clients who don't have a strong inner sense of who they are or cannot witness their own experience.

Clients who can't be mindful and follow their inner awareness are not good candidates for somatic interventions. Somatic psychotherapy and the use of mindful body awareness is based in the curiosity of wanting to inquire and learn from the body and mind. If that interest is not there, you can certainly cultivate it; but a basic human curiosity needs to be present before proceeding with these interventions. For example, a client struggling with body dissociations as a result of severe body trauma or body image issues, might not be ready to inquire into their body experience yet. If paying attention to the body feels too overwhelming or more anxiety producing, that would be a good indicator that somatic interventions are not right.

The use of safe touch is to be assessed very carefully in regards to the client's trauma background. A history that includes physical or sexual violation needs to be taken into consideration. It is better to err on the side of caution than to offer a technique the client will be overwhelmed by.

A good measure is tracking the client's awareness, curiosity and level of engagement with any of the exercises. If they are fearful, not open to the exploration, and not seeing any value, then this is a good indicator to re-assess.

CHAPTER 4
Guidelines and Safety

GUIDELINES FOR WORKING WITH THE BODY

1. **Inform the client when including body-oriented interventions:** Don't surprise the client with "new" techniques, but rather, explain what you are including.

2. **Choice and control:** Always ask permission, explain what interventions and exercises you are doing, and give options when possible.

3. **Resource safety:** Safety is of utmost importance. Find out what the client needs to feel safe (e.g., find a part of the body that feels good or strong and have the client periodically connect with this place by having the client imagine a safe place they can go to).

4. **Resource for wellness and strength:** Find somatic places in the body, therapy room, imagery, etc., that the client can associate with strength and wellness. Establish positive associations.

5. **Track for feedback:** How is your client doing? Is there dissociation or are they overwhelmed? If so, resource, slow down, or stop. Keep in verbal contact. If the client feels uncomfortable working with the body, stop and offer alternatives. Never insist on interventions the client does not want.

6. **Track for signs of physical safety:** (e.g., suicidal ideation, self-harm threads) and follow professional ethical guidelines.

7. **Be trustworthy:** Work within ethical codes, do not surprise clients, honor boundaries, stop when requested, be consistent and reliable, and be respectful at all times.

SAFETY FIRST - HOW TO WORK RESPECTFULLY WITH THE BODY AND MAINTAIN BOUNDARIES

Since working with body awareness can be new and can potentially bring up feelings of shame, discomfort, and trauma responses, you want to approach any body techniques with an open and respectful attitude.

Here are a few tips on how to view the body-oriented interventions in this book:

1. **Observe the client's response to any intervention suggestions:** Are they receptive, or is the client uncomfortable? If they are uncomfortable, don't proceed; instead, explore what works for them. Address any discomfort and ask, "What would make you feel safe?"

2. **Offer small, incremental changes:** For example, suppose that you want to work with a tightness in the body. Rather than suggesting a big change, you want to start with a small step such as: "How about you notice the tightness in the shoulder. What are you aware of?"

3. **Engage the curiosity of the client:** "What do you think of this tightness right now?" "How are you experiencing this sensation?" "What do you know about…?"

4. **Make the client the expert on their body:** "How does your body know that?" Refrain from telling your client what their body feels like or what they should do. This will only bring forth resistance, and your window of opportunity to have them explore the body-oriented ways of working will close.

5. **Respect physical and emotional boundaries:** When it comes to physical boundaries, assume that you want to keep a socially-appropriate distance unless you have discussed this topic with your client. (Please read Chapter 21 on the safe use of touch.) Be sensitive to cultural differences as well, since there are variants on how physical distance and closeness is perceived. Boundaries are not just physical, but also emotional. Be aware not to push anything on the client that they don't want to explore. You can offer or make them aware, but you want to assume the client's wisdom of their own body first.

6. **The client is the expert of their process:** That means reading their body cues of engagement and curiosity, and not being invested in your own agenda. Be flexible, and offer somatic techniques that put the client in the driver's seat.

7. **Somatic interventions only work if there is collaboration, curiosity, and an experiential mindset to learning:** Stay open and curious if your great intentions are being rejected. Find new and creative ways to work with the body that respect the pace and feelings for the client.

THE CLIENT'S BODY KNOWS BEST

Support the client's wisdom of their experience and process. This approach requires the experiential mindset of you, the therapist. Don't take rejection personally; be open and curious, even if an intervention does not work. The more present-moment focused you are, the more you will see what needs to happen, rather than what you think should happen. In this way, you can really listen to what the client is sharing about their body.

Some general guidelines:

1. Ask more about HOW an experience is feeling
2. Encourage curiosity more than solutions

Sample phrases that help facilitate body trust:

- "How are you noticing these feelings?"

- "Where are you sensing…?"

- "How are you experiencing this right now?"

- "As you are feeling this…what do you notice?"

- "How does the body experience of _____ appear to you in this moment?"

- "What are you curious about…now?"

- "What do you need right now to stay with this…?"

SOMATIC READINESS TIPS

These inquiry questions are a tool for the therapist to assess whether a client is ready to work somatically.

To what degree is my client able and willing:

1. To be curious about their body as a source of information?

2. To turn their attention inward and be mindful?

3. To stay inward and not pop out of mindfulness periodically to check back?

4. To engage with their quiet experience? (Do they get bored, switched off, irritated, self-aggressive or dismissive?)

5. To examine beliefs coming up such as: "Quiet is dangerous," or "If I am too inward I need to jump out," or "I can be overwhelmed, not seen"?

6. To explore their beliefs around "the body is not a safe place" and to be able to inquire into the deeper meaning of it?

7. To be in their bodies and explore other options?

If they are not able:

If a client can't be still and reflect inwardly, this may require that you teach them how to become mindful and be curious about the present-moment experience of their bodies before going deeper. Start this process using small practices and inducing mindfulness with guidance. Practice what it means to get quiet and stay inside.

The goal is to:

1. Get them used to turning inside.

2. Give them specific guidance on how to turn inside, and help guide them there and keep them there, in small steps.

HOW TO STABILIZE MINDFUL AWARENESS

- Observe for bodily signs of mindfulness, such as slowing down the breath and turning the attention inward, closing the eyes or downward-cast eyes.

- Look for signs of "coming out" of a mindful state, such as eyes fluttering, vigilant eye movement, unsettled body movements, or becoming more talkative and less reflective. You want to notice this "coming out" and gently guide them back towards mindfulness.

- Use reassuring language to normalize any fear of working somatically.

- Make contact in the "moment" of experience: "You just opened your eyes; you are not sure?"

- Stay calm and steady in your guidance. Slow down the experience so both you and the client can notice what is happening.

- The more slowed down and mindful you are, the more the client has permission to become internally focused.

THE THERAPIST'S TOOLKIT

CHAPTER 5
Self-Skills:
Prepared and Grounded

PREPARATION - SOMATIC AWARENESS IN YOUR OWN BODY

One of the key aspects of working somatically is preparing your body and mind for the work ahead. You want to be able to understand the techniques from the inside-out in order to understand their power and application for your client. In addition, you want to know your somatic baseline—a neutral zone from which you can feel and sense changes. For example, what accounts for your feeling of balance? How do you know when you are feeling balanced in your body and nothing is bothering you? What are the somatic markers that you can recognize in your body that tell you that you are tense, okay, relaxed, curious, etc.? How can you recognize feeling drained and deflated after working with a client? Have you "picked up" somatic information from a client that you are simply dismissing as tiredness? It's important to be somatically tuned-in to know the difference.

Knowing how you feel before you start your work gives you evidence, as well as a measure, to know what to do to balance yourself again. This is the most important assessment when learning to understand what burns you out and what rejuvenates you. Making awareness a basic practice so you know how you feel in your body, mind and heart, is part of the practice of a somatically-oriented therapist. It does not require a lot of your time; you just need a regular way to check in with yourself and sharpen your skills and awareness.

It can be helpful to cultivate a body-questioning vocabulary as part of your somatic work. The Taking a Body Snapshot for the Day Tool has basic questions you can ask yourself as you start your working day.

therapist exercise

Taking a Body Snapshot for the Day

PURPOSE

This exercise is designed to establish how you are today and in this present moment. Taking a quick inner inventory of how you are establishes a somatic baseline from which you can compare how you are doing while working with your clients throughout the day.

This snapshot is an inner-directed moment of awareness noticing yourself right NOW. Knowing your inner snapshot is critical; it makes you realize when you are off and when to come back to balance. You will be more inclined to notice when you are getting triggered, tired, overwhelmed or emotionally flooded.

You take a body snapshot to know where you are at and embrace it kindly. If you are having a vulnerable or bad day that is ok. Allow yourself to know how it feels in your body and own it. You are a dynamic process just like your client. Take the somatic snapshot and send a kind inner note to yourself. Be kind, stay open and get curious.

Tip: You can take this inner snapshot in-between clients, to help you stay tuned into yourself.

INSTRUCTIONS

- **How** is my body feeling today?
- **What** is the sensation of this _____ in my body right now?
- If this area (body part) could speak right now, what would it say?

therapist
exercise

Back-Body Awareness
for Therapy Readiness

PURPOSE

The back-body awareness in the therapist seat is a technique that can ground you as you get ready for a session or return you to your inner balance when you are feeling thrown off in a session. The goal is to reference an inner alignment of your back to access strength, balance and equanimity.

INSTRUCTIONS

Take a quiet five to seven minutes. You can do this before each session, or at the beginning of the day to get ready. Make sure you are undisturbed for that time.

Outer posture: Sit either in a chair or on the floor. Assume a relaxed, yet alert, posture by sitting upright and having your shoulders align with your hips. Make sure your head is also in this alignment and you are not protruding your chin. Slightly tuck your chin in; this will allow for an elongated neck in the back.

Align your posture so you feel upright. You can evoke an image that has a regal and relaxed quality to it. Close your eyes and check your inner posture by sensing this quiet, outer posture. You want to feel straight, and yet not braced in any way.

While working in the session:
You can use a simple reference of your back-body as you sit, and assume the relaxed but upright posture. The fact that you are reminding your body to sit this way will trigger a body memory of a relaxed and calm state. It is important to practice this posture several times prior, so that you can do a simple sitting and you will reap the benefits of a more relaxed state of awareness. It will allow you to shift into a more "big picture" perspective that can be helpful when you feel tired, bored, or stuck in your session. This simple body-awareness technique is best practiced in every session you can, so it becomes a healthy habit. Notice that when you are feeling tired or stuck, your body posture often mirrors this inner state.

Grounding Through the Body

PURPOSE

When you learn how to ground through your body, you can weather any challenge the client delivers.

Grounding through the body is a basic tool; use it often so you make it a healthy habit. You can somatically arrive in the body with your awareness regardless of if you feel disconnected, tired, activated or triggered. Learning how to ground is a basic health and wellness practice that will allow you to sustain your work. It also gives you a regular check-in with yourself on how you are doing. You can use this grounding technique any time before or after a session at work, or at home when you want to de-stress from your day. The purpose is to reconnect you with the joy in your work, your sense of well-being, and a calm mind and heart.

INSTRUCTIONS

First check in with yourself and then ground through the body. This can be done standing, sitting or lying down; modify it so it feels right to you.

Part 1:
Notice and check-in if you are:

- ☐ Tired
- ☐ Irritated
- ☐ Disconnected from your sense of joy or flow
- ☐ Triggered emotionally
- ☐ Sensory overloaded
- ☐ Re-hashing the last session
- ☐ Not feeling in your body
- ☐ Resistant to see the next client

Check what applies. Then take a breath and say: "It's okay; it's a rough day. This will pass. I now need to come back to my body."

Part 2:
- Take whatever posture feels comfortable for you. Since you have named your current feeling or body sense, take a breath and acknowledge where you are at.

- Tune your attention to go inside. You can have your eyes open or closed.

- Quickly scan what your body feels right now. If you are sensing irritation, see if you can identify "where" in your body you feel it.

- Place your hand on the body area. Take a breath and exhale slowly, melting the experience of agitation.

- Feel your feet on the ground. (If you are laying down, bend your knees and place your feet on the ground. This is preferable to stretching out the legs.)

- Gently push into your feet, as if you're doing a slow walk on the spot.

- Imagine you are pushing away the floor beneath you. There is a little exertion with this.

- Now imagine that your feet are planted barefoot in the grass or on the ground. Keep walking, pushing, and exhaling actively. Do this for two to three minutes.

- Then stop, pause and notice your body. Sense and see with your inner imagination the ground underneath you that is supporting you right now. Tune into that fact. It's not just imagination, it's also quite literal.

- Is there any change? How is your body now?

I feel_____right now.

I feel_____in my body.

I am letting go of_____.

I am grounding into_____.

therapist exercise

Shaking It Off (Laying Down)

PURPOSE

Shaking is a natural response the body uses to restore itself after it has experienced a fright or shock. You can use this body response in a conscious way to restore equilibrium and awareness.

This exercise helps connect the body with its inherent self-restoring capacity. This tool teaches you to safely release any tension or anxious feelings within the body. The goal is to interrupt any mental chatter and re-focus on the body. The motion "calls" body awareness back into the body. This would be a good practice when the client reports feeling "upset," "shaky inside," or ungrounded. You might feel vicariously triggered or ungrounded yourself by witnessing or facilitating the client's process. Use this exercise to re-establish your balance. The goal is to gently allow the shaking while at the same time feeling the connection to the ground.

INSTRUCTIONS

This is a four-to five-minute technique, and the goal is relaxation and grounding. In addition, you can use rhythmic music to facilitate the movement.

- You can do this standing up or laying down. If you lie down then place your feet on the ground for support. Knees bent and feet planted on the floor.

- Notice where the "shakiness" is in the body, by asking, "Where do I notice the shaky feeling right now?" Ask yourself: "What is the quality or rhythm of the shaky feeling?"

- Pay attention that the ground is supporting your back. Ask: "Can you notice the ground support?" Allow the ground to hold you.

- Follow up by exhaling gently and let the shaky feeling move into your feet, or the ground.

- Encourage natural breathing. Stay present with your body and your breath, let the breath slow down gently. If you are spacing out please open your eyes; you might have to sit up and change posture.

- Encourage a gentle pushing into the feet, this will create a rocking into the rest of the body. This step is a calming activity that should lessen the shaky feeling. You might have to notice a back and forth of "allowing the shaky" and then returning to the gentle rocking. It will take a few times to find rhythm. The goal is to ground the shakiness into a body rocking that allows self-agency and calming.

- Breathing facilitates the motion, so let it flow organically. Don't force your breathing; simply let it ride along with the movement.

- Focus only on the rhythmic motion; keep it consistent as you start to create a gentle pattern of motion.

- Pause the movement and notice the after-effect. Where can you feel and sense your body? What parts of your body are alive? Can you sense an inner motion? What is that like? How would you describe the feeling in your body now? Rest your body and enjoy your return to a balanced body state. You can use this practice to train your own activated states to return to a calming state. The more you practice this the more you will be able to make this a healthy habit for your therapist seat.

Note to therapist:

This is an exercise you can use with a client as well. If you do that be very mindful of any activation. Track carefully how the client uses this exercise. If the client becomes too activated, stop the movement. You are looking for a gentle release, not escalation. You might need to use shaking very carefully and have the client pause to notice what they are feeling. It is best to have them shake for a short while, then stop and observe their internal sensations.

Don't let the movement continue for longer than five minutes to avoid a trance-like state. Shaking is a biological movement and you want to ground the body, not dissociate it. The alternation between allowing the shakiness and then making the deliberate rocking motion will eventually ground the shaky feeling. Track carefully and mindfully for the changes and stay in good communication with your client. Make adjustments as you see them.

therapist
exercise

Calling the Internal Support Team

PURPOSE

This short exercise is to help you get ready to work. It's a visualization that centers your body and mind, and reminds you of the resources that you have in your life. When you are connected with your internal resources, you are able to be more present and available for your client. This exercise is especially helpful when you feel you need extra grounding for a session that you anticipate might be challenging. You can visualize this anytime you get stuck, don't know the next intervention to make, or just to ground yourself in well-being.

INSTRUCTIONS

This takes three to five minutes.

- Sit quietly and comfortably.
- Close your eyes and establish a centering breath into your body. Allow yourself to slow down and get ready to reflect.
- Complete the inquiry questions and know all who are on your team. (See inquiry questions in the section below.)
- Visualize these supportive people as a physical team sitting behind you in a semi-circle.
- Imagine them bringing to you their qualities that you admire. They are your personal team, rooting for your success and well-being.
- Notice what happens with your posture as they are sending their strengths to you.
- Open your eyes and notice how you are sitting right now.

Inquiry questions for establishing your internal team:

Who has been an unconditional support in your life? List three qualities/strengths you admire about this person.

1. _____

2. _____

3. _____

Think of three to five more people whom you admire. They can be alive or from another time. List three qualities about them that you admire.

1. _____

2. _____

3. _____

4. _____

5. _____

As you think of these people, list three aspects of yourself that you strive towards (e.g., you admire someone's grounded calmness and want to be more like them).

1. _____

2. _____

3. _____

Imagine this group of people taking a seat behind you in support of you. Notice what happens in your breath and body as you imagine them being behind you. Remember this team behind you as you work in your session. You can always call them up while you are working. It helps to have a physical marker in your body such as leaning back, or sensing the seat underneath you to somatically remember your team.

Self-Resourcing - Floor Work

PURPOSE

There are times when sessions are difficult, or you are tired and need a quick rejuvenation before seeing more clients. The quickest way is to connect with the ground and movement through the body. This exercise can be done anywhere between five to 15 minutes. Make sure you slow down, synchronize your breath with the movement, and follow the movement steps outlined.

INSTRUCTIONS

- Find a comfortable spot on the floor and assume a side position. Start on the right side, heart side up.

- Take a moment to feel the floor beneath you, allowing your weight to drop into the floor.

- Exhale your breath and empty out any tension you might feel.

- Now gently and slowly begin by moving your left arm from alongside the body towards the floor, as if you are dragging your arm gently across the floor; move it over your head and gently twist your upper body. Make this one continuous, fluid motion. The idea is to move the body into a twist that leaves the lower body where it is and only rotates the upper body by moving the arm overhead.

- When you can't move your arm anymore, begin the motion backwards—again dragging the arm over your head and alongside the floor until you come into the full side position again.

- Repeat this motion three to four times, or as time permits. Allow your breath to slow down with the movement. If you have areas of tensions in your body, you can gently pause and breathe into these tension spots.

- Switch sides. Start by laying on the left side now and begin to move your right arm from alongside your body towards the floor, gently across the floor, and then over your head until you come into a twist.

- It is important to keep the movement going—one long, fluid motion—and to allow any stretches that are occurring to be embedded in the motion itself.

- Rest on your side once you have finished and notice if your body is calmer and your mood has changed.

therapist
exercise

Somatic Inventory of Burnout Signs

"There is a soul weariness that comes with caring. From daily doing business with the handiwork of fear. Sometimes it lives at the edges of one's life, brushing against hope and barely making its presence known. At other times, it comes crashing in, overtaking one with its vivid images of another's terror with its profound demands for attention; nightmares, strange fears, and generalized hopelessness."

—Beth Hudnall Stamm, PhD

PURPOSE

Burnout or compassion fatigue can be associated with working closely with trauma and stress clients. In addition to the traditional burnout signs, this exercise lets you evaluate your burnout level from the inside-out.

Burnout is usually defined as a condition where the healthcare provider becomes emotionally and physically exhausted due to the job they are performing. These signs can be detected by paying attention to how the body responds. For more specific data, please consult the Burnout/Compassion Fatigue Inventory, ProQol, or the Life Stress Test.

Allow 20-30 minutes to go through this assessment. This is not just a list to check off, but an exercise to tune into your level of burnout distress on a somatic level.

Possible symptoms of burnout and compassion fatigue:

- ☐ Isolation from others
- ☐ Excessive blaming, feeling resentful
- ☐ Easily overwhelmed
- ☐ Stuck emotions that you are unable to express
- ☐ Irritability, tendency towards aggressive outbursts
- ☐ Frequent troubles with others, misunderstandings
- ☐ Compulsive behaviors
- ☐ Lack of self-care
- ☐ Nightmares, flashbacks of clients' stories or own trauma history
- ☐ Chronic physical ailments (gut health)
- ☐ Apathy towards life events, friends and work
- ☐ Difficulty concentrating

☐   Mentally and physically tired

☐   Preoccupied, or urge to distract (high use of media)

☐   In denial about problem

☐   Reluctant for change

☐   Lack of flexibility

☐   Lack of future vision

☐   Legal problems and indebtedness

☐   General negativity and depression

☐   Inability to complete tasks, feeling ineffective

☐   Somatic complaints that can't be explained (headaches, stomachaches, digestive issues)

☐   Lack of physical drive and energy

How to heal burnout/compassion fatigue:

- Kindness towards self

- Admitting the burnout problem and taking small actions towards health

- Compassionate body awareness

- Mindfulness moment and practices

- Awareness of the problem—admit the issue to self

- Sleep/Self-care

- Accept being on the path of recovery

- Listen to others who suffer

- Clarify boundaries for yourself of what works and what does not work

- Express your needs towards yourself first, then to others

- Get therapeutic help, or consult with people familiar with this issue

- Engage the physical body with somatic techniques and actions

- Take positive actions in your life

- Make a realistic plan and take small steps towards change that are sustainable

INSTRUCTIONS

Take a look at the previous list of symptoms. Do you recognize yourself? Check off the symptoms that apply to you. Notice your response to the list: Overwhelmed? Not sure where to start? Let's start with the body.

- Sit or lay down. Tune into your body. Close your eyes, feel your breath, take a moment to slow down first. One step at a time.

- Visualize one situation of burnout or compassion fatigue. You can call up a client that is draining or a session where you have felt disconnected or impatient to start sensing into the somatic experience of the burnout. What comes up?

- Now, tune into your body. Can you feel your body? What exactly do you sense in your body?

- Notice the source of agitation on a physical level. Let go of the story or the reason. Just focus on the body. Where is the location of agitation in the body right now?

- Make a quick body drawing to indicate where this agitation is located.

- Now imagine what the agitation is and what your body needs right now. Write down three qualities your body needs to overcome the agitation:

  1. _____

  2. _____

  3. _____

- Become quiet and see yourself applying these qualities. You can visualize, or move your body, bringing breath awareness to it. Notice what changes. Write down one positive statement of the change you noticed, or make a drawing of your body now.

CHAPTER 6
Therapeutic Attitude
When Working with the Body

EMBRACING AN EXPERIENTIAL VIEW

The experiential mindset is a growth-oriented mindset. The somatic psychotherapist allows themselves to see their work and the client's process as an open, changing, and dynamic process. When you reference this experiential mindset, you are allowing yourself not to be beholden to the client's narrative or their narrow perception of their problem. Rather, you entertain the perspective that there are many possibilities for resolution, and many paths towards healing.

It is human to have biases and pre-conceived opinions, but when you are working with the dynamic body, you need to be open to being surprised and changing what you had previously thought. With an experiential mindset, you are able to see a little deeper into the person, cultivate compassion, and create new options.

Being an experiential-mindset therapist means you are actively curious, open, and willing to experiment. For example, if the client wants to explore a hand movement and you suggest a way to explore it, but the client wants to explore the movement differently, can you include the expansion of the experiment? Just because you suggest a body experiment doesn't mean you need to stick to it. Once started, the experiment changes and evolves. The body does, too.

Here are a few hints about what it means to be of experiential mindset:

- Be open

- Be curious

- Allow for the experience of the client to guide you

- Don't be afraid to try things out

- Slow down—really slow down!

- Be in your own body; be mindful

- Allow for not knowing—it will refine the experiment

- Be kind to yourself, especially when you suggest something and the client says "no," or dislikes your suggestion

- Learn from your "failures"—make them teachable moments about the process (it's okay to fail!)

- Allow creativity and collaboration

- Follow what is meaningful and engaging for the client

- Become the scientist in real time, trying experiments and seeing where they lead

- Be open to surprises and what you have not thought of before

- Make sure you keep clear boundaries and safety

- It's okay to enjoy this phase of the work! Have fun with it!

Open Attention Technique

PURPOSE

Open attention is the non-judgmental awareness of "seeing what is." This is done with a curiosity of what is present in the moment—using your mindful awareness to sense what is present in 360 degrees. You are not "doing" anything, but simply sensing, noticing whatever there is.

This technique can be done to start an exercise or end an exercise. It is a crucial step in somatic work in order to set the right intention for what you are about to explore, as well as "harvest" what has been done. ("Harvesting" lets the client savor and linger in the aftermath of the experience.) This can be done with eyes open or closed. This instruction allows you to slow the client down and either get them ready for, or ground them after, an experience. What you are looking for is new insight, or how the client prepares to get ready. Open attention trains the mind and body to be with what is and develop emotional stamina. It lays the groundwork for accepting patterns of mind and body, and getting curious to explore them.

When to use open attention with clients:

- When you are about to experience an exercise and the client is apprehensive, nervous or needs to slow down.
- When you have done an exercise and want to see the effects of it. (This is the "harvesting" aspect of the exercise.)
- When they have tried something new, such as a new breath pattern or movement, and you don't want to miss its effects.
- When focus gets too narrow, open attention can open up perceptions. (This is important when tightness is experienced, anxiety arises, etc., as this exercise reestablishes trust in the body.)
- When you're focused on a somatic piece of work and want to open the client's attention to include a wider focus: whole-body awareness: "Notice how your entire body is participating right now; what else is there right now?"
- When a session has ended, this can be used as an integration technique. This will open the client towards appreciation and self-kindness and acceptance of their experience.

Therapeutic reasons:

- Opens the client's attention so they do not get stuck on pain or a narrow focus and meaning of their experience.
- Lets you invite the client into intensity without being overwhelmed.
- Allows for sensations and emotions to arise and not to be judged.
- Helps clients arrive in the beginning of an exercise.
- Teaches the value of a sensate focus in the body—clients learn to trust what is there and to be okay with what comes up.

- When a client is surprised by what comes up, you can ground them in open attention to allow them to have time to be with the experience.
- Teaches clients to linger with the experience and not to jump out too quickly. (This exercise interrupts the tendency to be "done" with it.)
- Provides an integrative function at the end of the session to honor what has occurred.

INSTRUCTIONS

This is done in three to five minutes.

- Allow your attention to be 360 degrees right now. If you could look around inside yourself in a slow, 360-degree way, what would you see there?

- Let this roaming attention be open, soft and all-inclusive.

- What else do you notice right now? Can you widen your attention to include what else you can notice?

- Go ahead and sense your entire body, not just the area you were focusing on.

- If you could zoom out right now and include all of your experience, what would you notice?

- Just be: see if you can drop any focus at all. Just be for a moment. Rest in the openness. *(Therapist, you may want to wait a few moments before asking the next question.)*

- What catches your interest right now? What is curious to you?

- Are you aware of any new insights or aspects?

Focused Attention

PURPOSE

Focused attention uses the attention capacity to sense, feel and witness one's experience, but places the spotlight on one area of inquiry. Focused attention cultivates mindfulness and stability of awareness. It helps the client stay with their experience and deepen into it. This is helpful when you are exploring sensations and emotions, and it allows for a process to occur. To focus in your attention engages the medial prefrontal cortex of the brain. This is impactful in gaining productivity and creating neuronal pathways to help reduce emotional activations. Learning how to focus is a way to help stress, trauma activations and emotional regulation. Focused attention is used in meditation practice as one way to cultivate a calm focus. It trains the mind to be steady and not to wander.

When and why to use with clients:

- Use when the client is distracted and jumps around by talking or not being able to focus well.

- If the client complains of not getting in-touch with what is underneath, the focused attention will help re-focus.

- This activity cultivates the ability to stay in process and trust difficult places to move on or dissolve.

- It teaches the value of here and now.

- It also teaches the value of process as it unfolds on its own.

Therapeutic reason:

It can be difficult for the client to "stay with" their experience when an emotion gets stronger, or an unpleasant experience is happening. This is when the therapist needs to "shepherd" the focused attention to stay in place. You want to gently encourage the client to see their focus without being overwhelmed, but also have the courage to explore what is unknown so they can discover something new.

INSTRUCTIONS

This is done in three to five minutes.

- Let your body be alert and open.

- Assume a posture that is upright and relaxed, but has a subtle effort to it.

- Turn your attention inward to the body.

- Cast your eyes down or close them. Make sure you can be alert and not sleepy.

- Connect with your attention. If you drift, come back. (This might happen many times.)

- Allow your attention to be focused right now. You can make the object of your focus the breath, a sensation in the body, a feeling, image or thought. Choose one. *(If you, as the therapist, have been working with one of these categories, you can suggest it.)*

- Settle into this one aspect. Now focus your attention right there, and see if you can keep it there.

- "Stay with it."

- Allow yourself to deepen and keep focusing. The experience might change slightly.

- Keep your attention focused until there is a shift or your attention wants to move on.

- Make sure you are not moving on because you want to avoid, or are bored—those are reasons to come back.

- Once the focus is completed, you naturally want to open up and see what else is there. What moves you naturally into open attention?

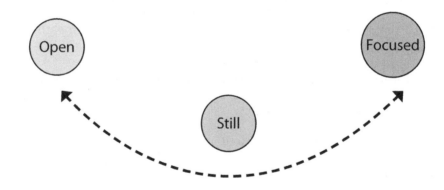

client
exercise

Moving Between Open and
Focused Attention

PURPOSE

The movement between the two attentions is a tool to help facilitate the natural rhythm of attention. Open attention is the ability to stay open; focused attention is the capacity to stay with an experience. The still point rests between the two attentions and serves as a neutral awareness.

When and why to use with clients:

- When the client can't deepen into the focused attention and gets easily distracted.

- When the client can be with the open attention.

- When the client experiences a stress or trauma activation, the movement between open and focused attention will help settle the arousal.

- If the client needs emotional regulation.

INSTRUCTIONS

This is a five-minute exercise. This exercise is different than the open and focused attention exercises because this one asks the client to quickly shift between two attentions. It's important to facilitate a smooth, but quick transition between the different attentions; it's about the "movement" of awareness.

- Start with one attention. Let your attention be as wide as possible.

- Draw your attention inward. You can have your eyes open or closed.

- Now move your attention to a place in the body, or an image or a feeling you want to explore. Take a breath and stay for a moment. (It's a full breath cycle, in and out; take a breath in between, before you move on.)

- Now move your attention again to a more open, diffuse attention, as if you are looking all over your internal body. Take one breath here.

- Move back to the focused place. This might have shifted or it's deeper. Take another breath here.

- Let yourself move back and forth with a full breath cycle.

- After a few breaths, you might notice a still point in-between—almost as if there is a breath in between the other two. Take that one. Just be. It's a moment of rest.

- You can now resume the back and forth movement, and it will be slower, as if you are swiping from a focused place in the body, to a resting moment, then back to an open attention that is located all over the body. Find a rhythm that works for you. (Most people want one to two breaths at each point.)

- After a few minutes, you will notice that you want to rest more; let that happen. There is a natural ending point in which the attention does not want to swing anymore. Follow the wisdom of your attention-body.

- Notice what has changed!

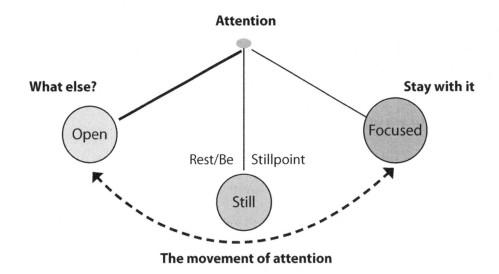

CHAPTER 7

How to Facilitate the Somatic Process

THE QUESTION WE NEVER ASK

"Why" questions have one big problem: They give you intellectual, pre-fabricated, habitual answers. These answers are not considered or coming from direct present-moment experience. "Why" questions foster a "knowing attitude," not an inquiry attitude.

When working somatically, you want inquiry, curiosity and open-ended self-discovery leading to empowered knowledge. The body is a mysterious, always unfolding experience—there are no right answers. Safe discovery leads to insight and good decision-making based on real-lived knowledge.

Rather than "why," ask: How, where, what is that like for you?

Don't ask for answers, ask for inquiry.

"Let's Experiment!
Would You Like to Try Something?"

PURPOSE

Direct Experience vs. Thinking About It

Inspire the client toward an experiential attitude in exploring their somatic experience. This goes two ways: The therapist's openness to try some new experiment also needs an open and unbiased mind. To explore the soma, you need to stay open to and curious about what wants to emerge and what wants to happen.

INSTRUCTIONS

Here are some inquiry questions that can be helpful:

- **What quality does it have?** What kind of joy, anger, sadness, etc., is it that you are feeling towards him/her?

- **What is the texture?** How do you notice this change right now?

- **Where is the location?** Where do you feel that tightening in your body?

- **How is it? Compare:** Is it trying to hold something in or let something out? Is it stronger on the right or left side? *(Note that the answer to this second question is probably irrelevant, yet it serves to guide a person more deeply inside.)*

- **What kind of movement?** What kind of movement goes with that feeling?

- **Where is the impulse?** What impulses are connected with this anger, sadness, etc.?

- **Notice what memory:** What does this feeling in the body (joy, anger, sadness, etc.) make you remember?

- **What kind of words?** What words go with this experience right now?

- **What kind of meaning?** If your fingers were talking right now, what might they be trying to say?

Making Empathic Statements

PURPOSE

The client's experience needs to be received by the therapist in ways that demonstrate that the client is acknowledged and heard. The most fundamental way we connect is through empathic knowing. To validate and make the client more receptive to their own internal experience and study of their body, we need to "pick the client up where they are at."

The statements provided below are sample statements to help make an empathic connection and ease the client into their own curiosity to study their body experiences. These statements need to be present-centered and focus on the experience at hand. Past-tense statements will draw the client into their memory or thought process.

When you want to facilitate the somatic process, you need to stay close to the body, as well as the present moment; otherwise, the client will not enter their body experiences.

INSTRUCTIONS

- Make present-moment statements
- Keep the statements short and concise
- Use statements that match the client's experience

Practice the sample statements below and then reflect on your style of naming the client's experience. Do you ask questions? Do you overstate? Do you have too much silence? Do you comment? Do you give advice?

In order to elicit the somatic process, you need to honestly reflect on your style and make changes. The language of the body is not to be revealed in questions, but in an open, warm and curious manner. These empathic statements reflect and invite the client to open up to their own experience. The goal is to be, and demonstrate, understanding!

Sample empathic statements:

- "You seem ____(sad, angry, anxious, etc.)."

- "You have a lot going on right now…"

- "There appears to be quite a lot of ____(emotions, sensation, thoughts, feelings) with…"

- "So, there is a lot of ____(energy, movement, etc.) right there…"

- "That can be hard to figure out…"

- "There's something curious about this right now…"

- "It seems like a lot of _____(emotions, thoughts, etc.) with…"

- "I sense that something challenging is coming up…"

- "That would be pretty upsetting…"

- "So, the sensation is moving right now…"

- "You are noticing the…"

- "That is painful for you…"

- "Ah, that makes you angry…"

Asking the Right Questions

PURPOSE

Asking questions can be utilized when you want to connect to a deeper meaning and observe the bodily experience. Often, questions are directed at understanding or are solution-focused. But in the somatic context, asking questions facilitates a further exploration and knowing, from the inside-out, of what is occurring and what can be explored in the process. Avoid the solution-focused questions and direct your questions in an open-ended way so the client needs to go to the body to find the answers. The "right" questions are those that connect the client with the answers they don't know yet, but have yet to discover.

INSTRUCTIONS

Notice the difference between: "Are you sad?" versus "What kind of sadness is this?"

Are you sad? - - - - - - - → I will answer from what I know, what you want me to answer, or what I think you expect. The answers will be from my head, not my body!

What kind of sadness is this? - - - → I have to feel, sense and go to my body to actually find out. I will take a moment, tune in, be mindful and find the answer as I inquire. I am now connecting with my body!

Sample questions:

- "What kind of (sadness, fear, confusion, numbness) is here?"

- "How deep does that tension go?"

- "Is there a texture that goes with that?" (E.g., emptiness, tiredness, constriction.)

- "Is there something familiar about this?" (E.g., tingling, intensity, weariness.)

- "Is there an image that goes with that?"

- "If this _____ had a color, what would it be?"

- "What sound would this _____ make?"

- "What is on the other side (behind, all around, underneath) it?"

- "What's happening in the rest of your body?"

- "How comfortable/uncomfortable/pleasurable is it?"

Guiding into the Soma

PURPOSE

Asking your client to STAY with an experience will aid them in exploring their present-moment experience.

Simple formula to connect and deepen the current experience:

1. Tune in (to present experience)

2. Stay (with present moment)

3. Explore (what is)

4. Notice (what has changed)

5. Reflect (on what's new, different or has meaning)

Use these directives (note: your tone of voice needs to be inquisitive and open):

- "Get curious about …"

- "Allow yourself to turn toward your **experience** right now." *(You can say "pain," "anxiety," "heaviness," etc.)*

- "What happens inside you when you say that?"

- "How do you experience that in your body?"

- "Go ahead and stay with this…"

- "Just notice your experience right now…"

- "Stay with that."

- "Stay with the _____ and see where it takes you."

- "See what the _____ knows…"

Example of one cycle of guiding the client into their sensory-emotional experience:

Set up: Client describes sadness.

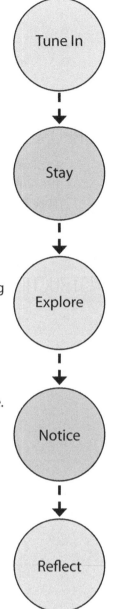

- **Therapist:** Allow yourself to tune into this sadness right now.

  Client: It feels heavy in my chest.

- **Therapist:** Stay with that quality in your body right now.

  Client: It's really heavy and sad.

- **Therapist:** Explore this heavy and sad mixture and see where it takes you.

  Client: It gets stronger and I feel tearful.

- **Therapist:** Notice what wants to happen.

  Client: Tears.

- **Therapist**: Very tender, huh? Go ahead and sense into how this is changing right now.

  Client: Yes, it feels like I am releasing the heaviness.

- **Therapist:** Does it seem easier to be with the feeling?

  Client: Yes, the heaviness is lifting. Still some sadness, but not as oppressive.

Guiding the Client into Their Somatic Experience

Give gentle directives with these simple statements:

Tune in…

Stay with…

Explore…

Notice…

Reflect…

After you walk your client through, you can start again with "Tune in… to what is changed now." "Stay with that change…" and so forth.

What Else?

PURPOSE

Facilitating a somatic unfolding means we need to follow the organic process. After you feel into the present-moment experience with mindfulness and body awareness, ask the question: What else? This is NOT to get an answer, but to facilitate an opening into the somatic present-moment experience. Ask this question, then see; ask again and see again. Notice what comes up. Where is your attention? What do you notice? Images? Feelings? Insight?

INSTRUCTIONS

- Become mindful.
- Close or open your eyes; take a breath to feel your body.
- Ask the following questions:

1. **What else?**

   What do you notice?

2. **What else?**

   How do you notice it in your body?

3. **What else?**

   What do you notice in your overall experience?

4. **What else?**

   As the therapist, notice that the "what else" questions are part of the experiential mindset. You can ask this question at different times in the session, but in particular when the client is exploring an unfamiliar body sensation and feeling.

   You use the phrase "what else" do elicit an unfolding experience. You don't want to overuse this, perhaps 3-4 times until you have the client get more body information they can get curious about. Now reflect on what came up. What did you discover? What did your body tell you?

client exercise

Listening to the Body

PURPOSE

Listening to the body is a fundamental tool to learn. This exercise can be done at many different times:

1. In the therapy session, as a tool for inquiry.
2. As homework, to practice getting to know the inner landscape of the body.
3. Whenever strong experiences arise, as a tool to self-regulate.

When you feel the need to practice listening into the body, take an inventory of what you notice and what compels you to turn inside. Then practice the listening technique. Afterwards, take another inventory and see what you have discovered. Because the nature of our inner experience can be fleeting to keep and experience, a log can be helpful over time.

I want to listen to my body because I notice:

_____

_____

_____

_____

INSTRUCTIONS

- Settle into a comfortable position, either sitting or lying down.

- Connect with the chair, or the ground you are laying on. Ground your body first with your breath.

- Do a quick scan though the body, noticing the obvious things such as tension, temperature, and anything else that stands out right way.

- Now open your attention as if you are casting a wide awareness throughout the body.

- Notice your body in a global and soft way. Rest your attention on areas of interest. For example, if you notice your heart region seems numb or closed, you can rest your attention here and wait. See how things shift by just paying attention.

- You can work through several areas of the body in this way. Don't do more than three areas in one sitting.

- If you have a question or inquiry you are sitting with in your life right now, you can bring it up in your mind's eye. Make sure you don't problem-solve or entertain details. It is best to ask simple questions.

- Now notice how your body responds. Does your body open, contract or is it neutral? Stay with what comes up.

- If you have emotions during this exercise, let them be there and notice that simply listening makes a change.

- If you have some insights, make sure you write them in your experience log.

Experience Log

Log your experiences when you listen to your body. Pay attention to when, and how, changes show up. What is different each time? What is the same? Are there repeating themes?

Day	My Body Feels	My Body Senses	My Body Story Is	Notes

CHAPTER 8
Tracking Tools

WHAT AND HOW TO TRACK THE BODY

"Tracking is noticing all the little things that go on while someone is talking, especially the things that aren't being talked about. It is knowing how to read these as clues to the speaker's present experience and meanings.... The therapist has this two-fold task: to be in the world of the client, in all the usual ways, and at the same time, to be outside that world, able to see it from a wider perspective."

—Ron Kurtz

Tracking, or noticing, is done by the therapist. For the client this would translate into noticing their inner experience. Tracking is the act of noticing the outward signs of internal experience. It is the observation of behavior, movement and expression that can give insight to what the client is experiencing. Tracking is not about interpretation, but rather about gathering clues that can guide the clinician to a more accurate understanding of the internal world of the client. It is very important to stay current to what you are tracking and check out in real time what you notice is correct and matches the experience of the client.

"Tracking" is a term borrowed from the animal world. When we track the imprints of animals, we can make educated guesses about them. By noticing the depth of an animal imprint, for example, an experienced tracker can estimate the weight and perhaps the mood of the animal, such as if it was hurried or on the run. Based on clues the animal left behind, a tracker can make a close guess about the life of this animal.

This metaphor extends to us tracking body cues. Noticing a calm and steady eye contact might indicate a curious and open engagement. On the other hand, a hurried look that is vigilant could perhaps indicate an internal state of fear. By tracking/noticing these cues, the therapist has an indication of what is happening for the client. This information can then help a therapist be more effective and accurate in offering therapeutic interventions.

Learning how to track is beneficial for the health of the therapeutic relationship. That's because it enables the therapist to become more attuned to the client's inner state, as well as increases the client's sense of safety and awareness. In short, the more aware the therapist becomes of the body cues, the more sensitive they will be with their somatic interventions.

Tracking means:

- Receiving information as it is, refraining from interpretation
- Relaxing our perception to see what is occurring in the present moment
- Noticing the subtleties of expressions
- Being mindful of what is being noticed and willing to be wrong with any conclusions

Who tracks whom?

- Therapist tracks client to gather information

- Therapist tracks themselves to stay present and self-aware

- Therapist tracks therapeutic relationship to notice what and how changes occur in the relationship

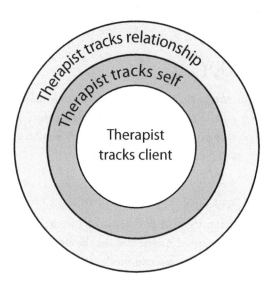

therapist
exercise

5 Kinds of Tracking

PURPOSE

When we track the client's experience, we are training ourselves to see behind the presentation of the client. We want to understand the meaning and hidden messages which the client is not fully aware of.

For example, you may notice that the corners of a client's mouth are turned down, there is a dull expression in their eyes, and their shoulders are slightly rounded and coming forward. The lack of eye contact might lead us to believe the client is disappointed, sad or resentful. That is the first layer of tracking the cues and making an educated guess. Now you track the tone of voice and you might notice that the person has a labored speech pattern, as if it is difficult to talk. What kind of hypothesis are you making now? Perhaps you speculate that the client is sad and burdened in some way.

However, you also observe that their voice is upbeat, almost manic in a staccato rhythm. By tracking these cues, you notice there seems to be a dissonance between them. How does this fit together? They are opposites: upbeat voice with a sad facial expression. What kind of hypothesis do you come up with now? One question I ask myself in these dissonant moments is: What wants to be expressed here and can't?

There are five types of tracking:

1. Tracking the content—how the story is being told.
2. Tracking the body's expressions and cues.
3. Tracking the autonomic nervous system cues.
4. Tracking the meaning behind the narrative.
5. Tracking what is not being said (the non-verbal story).

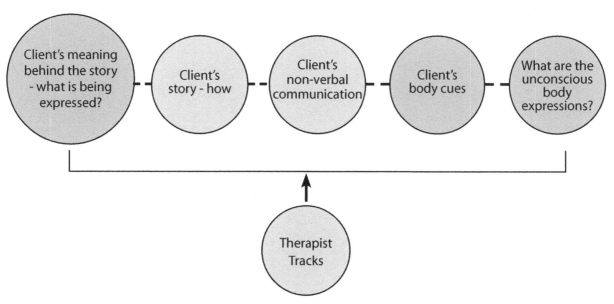

INSTRUCTIONS

Inquiry questions to ask yourself:

- How does that client present himself or herself to you?

- What is the official story?

- What is not being said?

- What is the meaning behind the story?

- What is congruent?

- What is incongruent?

- What is the body telling <u>AS</u> the client recounts their story?

- How is the body non-verbally responding? Breath, movement, speech pattern etc?

Tracking the Body Checklist

POSTURE

☐ Upright
☐ Collapsed
☐ Shoulders back or forward
☐ Slumped
☐ Tight and stiff
☐ Expanded and puffy through chest

☐ Holds arms and legs
☐ Curved spine
☐ Legs tucked, crossed
☐ Expressive, lots of moving
☐ Pulled in, contracted

TENSIONS

☐ Jaw
☐ Shoulders
☐ Around the eyes
☐ Back of the neck

☐ Belly
☐ Back
☐ Arms and legs

EYES

☐ Direct eye contact
☐ Averting eye contact
☐ Blinking
☐ Blank stare
☐ Sleepiness
☐ Logging expression
☐ Scanning, vigilant
☐ Scanning, fearful

☐ Dilated pupils
☐ Curious and open
☐ Tears
☐ Sparkly
☐ Warm and affectionate
☐ Tight corners of eyes
☐ Fixed stare
☐ Inviting

FACIAL EXPRESSION

☐ Facial tone—relaxed
☐ Quick flashes of emotions across the face
☐ Facial expressions very emotive
☐ Micro-expressions (flashes of fear, anger, sadness, genuine grief that move quickly across the face)
☐ Squelched expressions (smiles with a grimace)
☐ Tilt to the chin

☐ Facial tone-tense
☐ Facial expressions frozen
☐ Nods
☐ Smiles, genuine and not
☐ Emotions (anger, grief, sadness, contempt, excitement, joy, distress, fear, surprise)

GESTURE

- ☐ Fidgeting hands
- ☐ Sitting on hands
- ☐ High animation/gesturing while talking
- ☐ Punctuating with gestures while storytelling
- ☐ Folding hands
- ☐ Pointing
- ☐ Self-touching
- ☐ Reaching out for touch
- ☐ Holding objects

MOVEMENT

- ☐ Active
- ☐ Still
- ☐ Restless
- ☐ Upper body movement
- ☐ Lower body movement
- ☐ Repetitive movements
- ☐ Controlled
- ☐ Spontaneous
- ☐ Jiggling of feet or legs
- ☐ Jerky, abrupt
- ☐ High energy
- ☐ Low energy

VOICE

- ☐ Loud, strong
- ☐ Weak, quiet
- ☐ Little emotion
- ☐ High emotional tone
- ☐ Low emotional tone
- ☐ Rapid
- ☐ Labored
- ☐ Staccato rhythm
- ☐ Singing, lulling quality
- ☐ Harsh quality
- ☐ Squeezed voice
- ☐ Childlike voice

SPEECH

- ☐ Slow, deliberate
- ☐ Speedy
- ☐ Brief
- ☐ Redundant
- ☐ Sparse
- ☐ Punctuating
- ☐ Patterns, tics ("*you know.*")
- ☐ Pauses
- ☐ Trails off in their thoughts as they are telling the story
- ☐ Rapid speech firing, no pauses in between sentences
- ☐ Thoughtful

BREATH

- ☐ Held in upper chest
- ☐ Ebb and flow throughout the front of the body
- ☐ Held in belly region
- ☐ Big inhale
- ☐ Big exhale
- ☐ Squeezed breath
- ☐ Gasping while talking

PRESENCE

- ☐ Alert
- ☐ Sleepy
- ☐ Absent
- ☐ Distracted
- ☐ Dissociated

therapist
worksheet

Tracking for Trauma Cues

PURPOSE

When you track the body for information or cues, pay special attention to any signs that a trauma arousal is present. Tracking for trauma cues is the best indication that your client is getting emotionally overwhelmed, agitated, or beginning to freeze and dissociate.

Reading these cues early and accurately is important, as you have a therapeutic intervention choice to make. When the client is becoming anxious, overwhelmed, or freezing to the degree that they can no longer be present with their experience, you want to aid the client towards safety and resource.

Trauma cues are organized as hyper-arousal and hypo-arousal, indicating the spectrum of trauma arousal. Please note: These are body cues and need further assessment to make a full diagnosis. These tracking cues are in support of other trauma indicators.

Track for these cues and determine what your next therapeutic step is. Check all that apply.

HYPER-AROUSAL CUES

EYES

- ☐ Eyes widening (as if in shock)
- ☐ Eyes searching and scanning (vigilance)
- ☐ Eye contact direct and threatening
- ☐ Eye contact sustained with conflicting emotions (staring)
- ☐ Eye contact with confused look

SKIN

- ☐ Skin flushed
- ☐ Sweat pearls on forehead
- ☐ Tingling sensations on skin (reports pins and needles)
- ☐ Skin appears patchy (red blotches on neck and chest and parts of face)
- ☐ Client self-reports hot, itchy skin

EMOTIONS

- ☐ Anger flashes and irritation
- ☐ Crying easily

- ☐ Emotional affect high and quickly aroused
- ☐ Jumpy, jittery, looks nervous
- ☐ Vigilant to every sound in the room
- ☐ Vigilant to every movement in the room

BODY

- ☐ Reporting inner heat rising in the body
- ☐ Clammy hands and sweating
- ☐ Body movement erratic or abrupt (motor functioning impaired)
- ☐ Reports stomach flutters (butterflies)
- ☐ Reports taste changes (for example: metal)
- ☐ Ringing in ears (or tinnitus gets stronger)
- ☐ Various muscle tensions (shoulders, belly, arms, hands, legs)
- ☐ Body contorts into involuntary leaning postures and twists

MIND

- ☐ Memory loss/gaps
- ☐ Mind races and reports lots of details
- ☐ Attention is hyper-focused
- ☐ Reports intrusive memories or imagery

HYPO-AROUSAL CUES

EYES

- ☐ Eyes dull and withdrawn
- ☐ Eyes have a blank, fixed stare
- ☐ Eyes rolling back into head
- ☐ Eyes have a vigilance that is hidden (takes peeks, afraid to look)
- ☐ Eye contact quality is disrupted, can't sustain, or sustains for a long time

SKIN

- ☐ Skin gets pale (lifeless quality)
- ☐ Client self-reports cold skin
- ☐ Cold sweat
- ☐ Client self-reports tightness

EMOTION

- ☐ Numbness of feelings/sensations
- ☐ Flat affect
- ☐ Feelings are disconnected from body (reports cut off in body)
- ☐ Can't report sensation, jumps to meaning-making and analyzing
- ☐ Reports being "blank" or "nothing"

BODY

- ☐ Quality in body tone is held or lifeless
- ☐ Restricted body motions
- ☐ Crying, collapsed body (chest, belly)
- ☐ Overall muscle tension (deep internal muscles and tendons, holding tension)
- ☐ When asked to report experience, can't sense or feel own body
- ☐ Reports body numbness
- ☐ Feels overwhelmed or too confused to sense the body
- ☐ Speech listless, repetitive with a flat tone

MIND

- ☐ Memory loss, substantial time gaps
- ☐ Confused mind (time sequence off—in extreme fugue states)
- ☐ Attention impairment, delayed responses
- ☐ Delayed, slow responses in dialogue
- ☐ Avoids painful memories

Tracking My Body Chart

INSTRUCTIONS

Identify a body part that you want to learn more about. For example, it could be that you carry tension in your shoulders, or you notice that your belly is clenched a lot.

My body part to work with is:

_____

Today: The way I view my body is:

_____

After five days, summarize what you have learned. This chart provides you with a visual aid and concentrated data about what happened as you placed more awareness on your body in a sustained way.

How do you feel about this body part now?

_____

What has changed?

_____

What changes in your awareness made the difference?

_____

Make a new statement about how you feel about this body part today.

_____

Tracking My Body

client worksheet

	Day 1	Day 2	Day 3	Day 4	Day 5	Notes
How I **think** about my body part						
How I **feel** about my body part						
What triggered me today was…						
What helped was…						

Tracking My Body

client worksheet

	Day 1	Day 2	Day 3	Day 4	Day 5	Notes
I neglected my body in these ways today……						
I changed one thing today						
I looked at my body and I saw…						
When I close my eyes and sense my body I notice……						

INTEGRATING SOMATIC THERAPY TOOLS IN PRACTICE

CHAPTER 9
Mindfulness and Body

"Relax your judging mind, feel your body now. The good news is that you are present, the bad news can be that you can feel what is truly going on. What is even better—now you have a choice of what to be."

—Manuela Mischke-Reeds

WHAT IS EMBODIED MINDFULNESS?

Mindfulness orients the client internally to the ebb and flow of present-moment experiences. The non-judgmental nature of observing is critical to understanding your internal experience and growing your emotional capacity to feel and sense without becoming reactive or overwhelmed.

The "here and now" training that mindfulness provides is critical when working with somatic experiences. Since emotions and sensations are entangled, it is easy to become sidetracked into the intensity of emotions or the disorientation that strong sensations can bring. You can watch the present-moment experience in the body and learn not to "enact" a trauma memory, but rather witness the experience.

Mindfulness, and in particular embodied mindfulness, provides a resourcing and stabilizing aspect to the therapeutic process. Every time the client slows down and pays attention to the body in the present moment, the brain and body are being trained towards observation. This observation process inhibits emotional activation and is achieved by the prefrontal cortex down-regulating any overwhelm, confusion, or emotional triggers.

PITFALLS WHEN WORKING WITH MINDFULNESS

There are times when working with mindfulness is not appropriate or can activate the client further. As with any intervention or technique, the clinician needs to track and assess its usefulness for the client. Here are a few pointers about what to look out for and when to discontinue using mindfulness:

Client's pitfalls:

- Can't stay in mindfulness: Can't observe present experience, but jumps into thinking. For example, the client thinks about an experience rather than being with it.

- Can't stay in mindfulness and dissociates. This is a clear indication that mindfulness is not helpful.

- Gets overwhelmed and flooded by internal cues; too much inner stimulation.

- Uncomfortable sensing and feeling the body. Not able to see this discomfort as a way to explore their experience but rather wants to push it away.

- Mindfulness and slowing down acts as a trigger. Going inside provokes traumatic memories the client can't handle.

- Gets lost for a long time in thoughts, confuses being mindful with analyzing thoughts.

- Mindfulness raises internal distress: Anxiety increases.

Therapist's pitfalls:

- Gets overwhelmed, triggered, and impatient with client's instructing and dissociating or inability to slow down.

- Wants to rescue or force mindfulness by mechanical leading too much.

- Too many techniques; guidance is too technical and not spacious.

- Not tracking the body cues accurately, making assumptions that slowing down is okay, when in fact the client is spacing out, or getting overwhelmed internally.

- Not maintaining one's own mindful presence; dissociates along with client.

REMEDY THE PITFALLS

- If the mindfulness instructions are neither deepening the client's awareness nor engaging their curiosity—STOP.

- If the client gets overwhelmed or is under-resourced, stop, talk about it, and create a resource first. (For more on resourcing, please refer to Chapter 23.)

- Make sure the client is willing and curious to try mindfulness.

- Take time to explain, set it up, and make sure you orient towards a purpose. What are you looking for? What is it like for you to not think and just be with no thoughts? How is it to pay attention to your body and not having to do anything?

- Try small amounts of time, such as one to three minutes, first before having the client go for a longer time.

- Always ask open-ended questions: How does this feel for you? What is your experience? What do you notice? What arises?

- If the client gets stuck, practice kindness and curb your disappointment. Being mindful of one's body and mind is not easy. It takes monks a lifetime of effort, discipline, and dedication to achieve equanimity and peace! Be patient and kind.

How to Induce Mindfulness

INSTRUCTIONS

There are two ways to induce mindfulness: You can guide the client through imagery or you can explore mindfulness through body sensation.

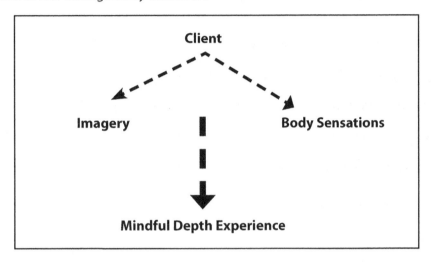

Imagery:

Use a soothing voice and describe a peaceful scene that the client will like. Ask them what they prefer: Ocean, woods, etc.

Script:

"Imagine going for a peaceful walk [through the woods, on a beach near the ocean, etc.]. You slow down your pace and take in the surroundings. Minding your step, you are filled with the serenity and peace of the nature around you. As you walk, you go deeper into a calm place. Your mind slows down, your thoughts are slowing down, and you are letting go of any busyness."

Use words/phrases such as:

- "See yourself walking slowly and mindfully…"

- "Look around and take in the peaceful environment…"

- "Imagine yourself fully in this favorite setting…"

- "Take in the beauty and calm right now…"

Body sensations:
Using a soothing voice, guide the client into their body sensations.

Script:

"Notice your body sensations right now. Feel yourself on the chair and feel how your body and weight make contact with the chair. Allow your breath to slow down. See if you can draw your attention into your body and be with the sensations right now. Allow anything busy or negative to melt away. Allow the extensions to melt, the thoughts to melt, and focus on the body sensations that are pleasant right now. Slow down the breath and feel into the body."

Use words/phrases such as:

- "Allow your body to feel…"

- "Stay with the sensations of pleasure, calm…"

- "Slow down and feel into the body right now…"

- "Notice how you can breathe calmly in this moment…"

- "Sense into your body…"

Inducing mindfulness depends on:

- Your tone of voice: Calm and steady

- Your pace: Slow and patient

- Your description: Short and precise

- Your flexibility: Tune into the client's particular preferences—don't stick to scripts that do not fit

- Your creativity: Add small nuances

- Your inner state: Be mindful yourself!

client exercise

Cultivating Self-Witnessing - Suspend the Moment

PURPOSE

An important skill in any of the somatic exercises is to witness oneself. The idea is to notice what is happening in the moment and in your body. You can witness your feelings, thoughts, sensations, movements and behavioral responses to people and situations. This skill is to learn how to self-regulate. Cultivating an inner witness is essential when you want to learn from your body. Suspend the moment frequently throughout the day. See what happens as you train in the art of witnessing your life.

INSTRUCTIONS

Practice suspending the moment by building in pauses before you do or act on anything.

Steps to practice:

1. Suspend: Hit the pause button on anything that you are doing right now.

2. Notice: What is happening in your experience right in this moment.

3. Track: How you are feeling your body right now.

4. Stay: Don't change anything, but stay present.

5. Continue what you were doing and see if you experience yourself differently.

Helpful questions to ask yourself:

- Where is my attention right now?

- How do I experience my body right now?

- What do I notice in my awareness right now?

This exercise needs to be repeated frequently. See if you can build this into your day.

client
worksheet

Befriending the Body

PURPOSE

This exercise is cultivating a basic kindness to your body. Go through the steps. You can repeat any of them any time. Befriending is a process. Be patient.

INSTRUCTIONS

Part 1: Before the exercise

Notice your body right now. What are you noticing? How do you feel about your body? If I would ask you: "How friendly are you towards your body?" What would you say? How would you describe your body in three words or phrases?

Steps for befriending the body:

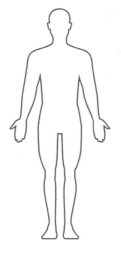

My body is:

1. _____

2. _____

3. _____

- Lay down on a comfortable surface where you feel supported.

- Relax the body as much as you can.

- Feel the gravity of the body and give into the support underneath you.

- Take three slow, sustained exhales and drop your awareness into your body and this present moment.

- Let go now and just sense and feel your body.

- Start with the back of your body: Soften the back as if you are melting into the ground.

- Continue with the front of the body and soften any tension.

- Take another three soft and sustained exhales and notice what is easier already.

- Now move your attention through the body. See what area of the body calls you. This can be a tension, an awareness, a place in the body you find challenging or a "feel-bad" area. Allow your ATTENTION to get you to the right place, not your thinking mind.

- Stay in this area of attention and apply some soft breathing, tender and gentle, like touching a beloved animal or person. Send a light, soft breath into this area of the body.

- Stay with your attention until you notice some change. This can be an opening of some kind, a change such as the tension melting.

- Then let go of the soft breath focus and see what is there now.

- NOW! Send a kind note to this area of the body. For example: "I welcome you. I love/ embrace you, too. Thank you." Make it short and sweet.

- Notice again and see what is changing right now.

- You can now allow your attention to move to another area of the body, or repeat the steps in the same area if you are still curious about what is happening there.

- Be open, curious and allow the change to happen.

Part 2: After the exercise

Now sit up or report laying down what you feel and sense. If I asked your body right now: "How friendly are you towards your body?" What would it say? Describe your body in three words or phrases.

Reflection of change:

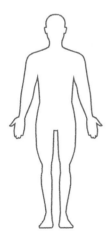

My body is befriending:

1. _____

2. _____

3. _____

Take a moment and reflect on what you can change after this experience. Make one small change that you can keep this week.

I want to treat my body_____

I want to change _____

The one commitment I make to my body this week is _____

Highlight the reminder note for the week:

I am befriending my body….

client
exercise

Relaxing Rest

PURPOSE

This exercise facilitates opening your body to a deep level of relaxation by not "doing anything." To fully rest in the body is not that easy. Usually we think we need to "do something," and "be productive," and we don't learn to trust the body. The body needs space and time to "talk" to you. Learning to truly relax and rest is to tune into the body on a deep level, rather than a thinking level.

INSTRUCTIONS

- Lay down on your back. Make sure you have a comfortable, supportive surface to lay on.

- Have your knees bent, feet flat on the ground.

- Rest your body completely into the ground. You can use a pillow underneath your knees, if you need more support under your legs. The same goes for the rest of your body—if you need more pillow support, you can accommodate your body.

- Rest your arms alongside your body or across the lower belly.

- Connect with your breath, and slow the breath down.

- Melt the body into the floor. Notice the tensions in the body and see if you can melt them by placing the breath in the area you are working with.

- Allow the weight and tensions to melt away.

- See if you can relax the hot spots of the body such as jaw, shoulders, belly, chest and legs.

- Melt and see the resting quality coming forth.

- Imagine a "lazy" animal, such a relaxing lion or a dog, and see yourself melting just as they do.

- Let go of any worry and thinking. If you are noticing the thinking, come back to the breath.

- Examine the "doing" parts coming up. When you notice that, respond by melting the body again.

- Allow yourself to be alert while you relax. If you get sleepy you can notice this and focus again on the back of your body and melting the body into the ground.

- Pay attention to how your body lets go and aligns naturally. Allow yourself to simply be here in your body without a goal.

Moving Body Scan

PURPOSE

The moving body scan is an essential tool you can repeat many times. The moving body scan is a great way to see where you are at somatically, as well as train your mindfulness of body. In this exercise, you will move very slowly and with "micro-movements," which should be barely visible from the outside. The goal is to inspire sensations by moving different parts of the body ever so slightly.

During this exercise, it is recommended that you sit or stand. Begin with the head and then travel down the body until you reach the toes. The overall quality of movement you are going for is slow, gentle and swaying. As you proceed through the exercise, notice what is happening in your body. If you could assign a temperature inside, what would it be?

INSTRUCTIONS

- Imagine being a gently swaying tree or being seaweed underwater.

- Now bring a small movement to your head. Let it ride on the vertebrae of your neck, gently rocking, swaying side to side.

- Allow your breath to travel to the areas you are working with. Go very slowly.

- Travel to the neck. This is an easy area to feel a side-to-side movement. Make small up and down movements.

- Allow yourself to relax completely.

- Track how the breath changes as you move this way.

- Move your awareness down to the shoulders and chest. Make small movements through the chest cavity.

- Follow your exhale, and how the shoulders drop.

- Stay for a few moments with the expansion and relaxation that arises.

- Travel to the belly and then to the back of the spine.

- Travel up and down the vertebrae of the spine. Each vertebra can be moved very slightly by creating a subtle micro-movement in the back. Experiment with what works for you. You might have to adjust how small or large the movement can be to feel right.

- Drop the effort here, relax into your body and work with what is there.

- Let your awareness move into the pelvic area and the legs. Pay attention to where the movements want to go. Allow the breath to be slow, as well.

- Include any other parts of the body: Feet, hands and arms. You might notice how there is a sense of your whole body moving.

- Continue for a few more moments. Just let the gentle swaying movement happen.

- Where and how do you experience the sensations?

- Breathe, relax, and let go of any effort. If you notice a tension, see if you can let it go.

- After a few minutes, let the movement come to stillness and track what is happening inside your body.

- Do you feel more in touch, more vibrant? Are there textures of feelings? Just let it be.

- Be with your experience without judgment. Sit and notice.

- Listen to your body with an open heart.

Reflection:

Before the moving body scan, I feel my body to be: _____

After the moving body scan, I feel my body to be: _____

Walking Meditation

PURPOSE

Walking meditation is a welcome break from a sitting mediation. It provides some variety, as well as another way to experience the body in motion while being mindful. This can be applied in daily life, such as when walking to the car, or a destination. For the therapeutic context, you can apply walking meditation in your office to help regulate strong emotion, ground a client's high arousal, and help move the body into more awareness.

INSTRUCTIONS

Walking helps to focus and center the mind through the single action of striding. The eyes are downcast and not focusing on anything. They are not searching or fixed on the environment—it's a soft focus. The feet step one at a time in a slow and mindful way. Give yourself 10 to 15 minutes of walking time. Set a timer to remind you so you don't get distracted by watching the clock.

- Start with a standing posture.
- Notice your back—straight, but relaxed.
- Feel your feet on the ground and connected with the earth. Take a deep inhale and center yourself first.
- You are walking, but you are not "getting anywhere." If you are in a small space walk back and forth. Adjust your stride to where you are walking.
- Cast your eyes downward in front of you; have a soft and receptive gaze. Make sure your posture stays upright and regal even as your eyes are downcast.
- Take one step at a time and become aware of how you place your foot each time.
- Each step, each foot moment touching the earth, is your practice of mindfulness.
- Let the breath be normal and flowing. You can synchronize it with your step, but it is best to have the breath be free.
- Notice your thoughts and let them go when they arise, gently labeling them, such as "hello thought" or "hello my friend." Then return to your breath and your walking.
- Make slow, deliberate walking motions. Make sure you have your full attention on your body. If not, you might end up going too fast or too slow.
- Get into a rhythm, such as: Lift your foot, step forward, shift your weight. Repeat this rhythm: Lift, step, shift….
- Stay close to your moving body; empty your thoughts and be with your walking body.
- After the time is up, stand for a moment. Close your eyes and notice your body.

Reflection:

Before my walking meditation I noticed in my body: _____

After my walking mediation I noticed in my body: _____

client
exercise

Simple Earth Mindfulness

PURPOSE

This exercise was designed after working with a client who said she was tightly bound and trapped inside. She could not trust anyone or open-up to anyone. She loved being in nature, loved the Earth, but could not trust people. When it is challenging to trust others, it can be helpful to work with trusting nature. This meditation reminds you to trust the Earth and connects you again with your own innate goodness.

INSTRUCTIONS

- Lie on the floor. (This can also be done reclining.)

- Consider the ground beneath the body.

- Conceptualize how the ground is holding you up. Think "the Earth is always there for me" or any other positive phrase that suits you.

- The heaviness you feel is gravity gently pulling you to, and holding you on, the Earth.

- Focus your senses on the back of your lungs.

- Let yourself breathe into the back of your lungs.

- Imagine the Earth is meeting you here.

- Then let the Earth breathe with you. Imagine the Earth is a giant lung breathing into your lungs, rejuvenating you.

- The Earth is kind, gentle, and taking her time to breathe with you and into you.

- Let the exchange between you and the Earth happen; allow your breathing to interact with the Earth's.

- Notice how you slow down, how your breath expands, how the belly softens.

- Notice how your mind slows and how your sense of well-being returns.

- Track your experience.

Reflection:

I trust the earth to_____

I trust my body to _____

CHAPTER 10
Body Awareness and Body Reading

Body awareness is basic to anybody's somatic practice. In order to work with the body and learn from our experiences, we need to establish a fundamental awareness—a starting and returning point—in order to keep track of what has changed. This is the basis of practice-evidence.

Since our experiences are highly individual and personal, we need to establish a baseline against which we can measure our experiences. Otherwise we will forget, or begin to taint our present experiential understanding with past experiences. How can we keep our attention fresh and engaging? How do we do it? Where do we start? What do we look for?

The body's self-knowledge is innate. The first awareness, before we begin any practice, is recognizing that the body is already self-aware. Busy with routine concerns, ideas, fears and preoccupations, we diminish our sensitivity to self-perception with thought clutter.

Here are some basic tips to start working with body awareness:

- Become aware of where you are "now"— that is your starting baseline. Feel free to write that down.

- Notice the gross and subtle. For example, you can note: "today I am tired," which is the gross level; or you can note: "my eyes are heavy and withdrawn," which would be a subtle level.

- Stay present and notice distractions. Notice when you tune out and what makes you tune out. Bored? Anxious? Coming close to something that is uncomfortable?

- Once you have gone through body awareness and reading, take another baseline. Check in on what is different, what has changed, and again notice the gross and subtle levels. You want to mark the changes, however small. It's in the incremental, small changes that big changes get unleashed. Stay tuned to the subtle level of the body awareness.

client
exercise

Global Awareness of Body

PURPOSE

Body awareness is basic to anybody's practice. In order to work with the body and learn from our experiences, we need to establish a fundamental awareness—a starting and returning point—in order to keep track of what has changed. This is the basis of practice-evidence.

We start with global awareness of the body. We do "nothing," and are aware through our senses of what the body is like in this moment and in the next. The trick is to stay awake and not fall asleep. If this concept is new to you, try starting with three minutes of focused awareness and then work your way up to 15 minutes. It is important not to doze off, or allow yourself to be distracted or retreat back into thought clutter.

By repeating this practice of global body awareness and following the instructions, you will strengthen your "awareness muscle." This then becomes the basis for any other somatic body practice, as you will have a good, solid base from which to start and return.

INSTRUCTIONS

These instructions are basic guidelines to help train your awareness to notice and trust the body.

- Set a timer. If you're new at this, start with three to five minutes and gradually increase the time until you can do it for 15 minutes. Although this seems like a very relaxed practice, it takes concentration and training. You are learning to sharpen your attention patterns.

- Get comfortable. It is best to lay down and support the body with pillows so that you are totally relaxed. You should not experience any discomfort at all. Take a moment to get it right.

- Make sure you are alert enough to be relaxed without falling asleep. If you notice that you're tired, it's better to limit this practice to three to five minutes with a timer so you can get the most out of the exercise. You don't want to use this practice to train yourself to fall asleep more efficiently!

- Say to yourself: "I am going to do nothing, just be with my body, and observe what it does."

- Close your eyes and exhale a couple of times.

- Allow your attention to roam throughout your body. Don't be systematic—for instance, don't focus your attention from head to toe. This is an awareness practice designed to allow yourself to observe what the body does randomly, and learn its inherent patterns of intelligence. If you focus your attention deliberately, it becomes a different kind of practice. This is about "doing nothing" and learning to observe what the body is already doing. Watch and learn!

- Take notice of which parts of the body are responding. For example, you might notice a shoulder relaxing, or how clenched the belly has been, or you might tune into the quality of your breathing.

- Allow your attention to roam—there is no system to follow. Become increasingly still in order to better observe your body from the inside-out.

- When the timer goes off, stretch your body and sit up. Don't allow yourself to doze off. Take note of how you feel in your body.

- Allowing for some transition time; you can write or reflect. Do you notice how your body is more sensitized?

HOW TO USE IN THERAPY

Guide your client through these steps. Start with one to two minutes to debrief with them. If they report that they can't stay with their body, or if they get distracted, you can coach them gently back to their awareness. This is an excellent tool to repeat at the beginning of each session. This will slow your client down and get them comfortable with learning how to read their body. Use it as a jumping-off point to explore and discuss issues and places in which the client is stuck or afraid to move forward.

Body Awareness Inventory

INSTRUCTIONS

Circle the ones that fit or add your own to describe your current experience.

pulsing	moving	pressure	prickly
calm	still	awake	yawning
burning	streaming	billowing	weak
strong	contraction	flowing	tense
twisting	rotating	restless	irritated
shivering	vibrating	trembling	quivering
pain	liquid	sleepy	pulling
hot	lengthening	cold	numb
pins and needles	relaxed	frazzled	at ease
shaking	breathing light	breathing strong	held
wringing	choking	pushed	wrapped
light	heavy	straight	crooked
loose	tight	bubbly	electric
agitated	alive	racing	blissful

Add your own descriptions in a sentence or image:

client
worksheet

Naming Your Present-Moment Experience in Your Body

PURPOSE

Develop your body awareness with this worksheet. This can be used in the session or as homework after a session.

INSTRUCTIONS

As you read through the following statements, fill in the blanks.

Right now I am feeling _____ (emotion) **and I am sensing in my body**_____, _____, _____(at least 3 body sensations).

I am curious about my body_____(name one sensation).

I am connecting with what is in my body_____
(name one curious aspect; what gives you pleasure) **and I am learning that my body shows me** _____ (describe a little detail).

I also notice my breath is _____ (be descriptive about what and how and where the breath is).

As I feel my overall body, I feel_____(what is coming to as you feel and sense your body?).

I can say that now I am _____ (current-moment experience).

client worksheet

Identifying Body Themes

PURPOSE

If your body could talk, what would it say?

This exercise moves you systematically through the different areas of the body and shows you what answers you get. This exercise helps identify the themes of your body that you already know about, in addition to the themes that are hidden. By tuning into the body in a mindful way, you can deepen the answers and insights you will get.

INSTRUCTIONS

Do an initial pass-through by asking the question regularly in your ordinary state of mind; then switch into mindfulness: Slow down, close your eyes and ask the question again. There might be a phrase, an image, or a word that comes up.

Body Area	If your body could talk, what would it say? *Ordinary State - What I know now.*	If your body could talk, what would it say? *Mindful State - What I know from the inside-out.*
Front of Body		
Back of Body		
Head		
Neck		
Shoulders- Back of Shoulders		
Shoulders- Top of Shoulders, Joints		
Front of Chest		
Heart Area or Center		
Mid-Back		
Lower Back		

Body Area	If your body could talk, what would it say? Ordinary State - What I know now.	If your body could talk, what would it say? Mindful State - What I know from the inside-out.
Solar Plexus		
Belly		
Lower Abdomen		
Pelvis		
Upper Thighs		
Lower Legs		
Knees		
Ankles		
Feet		
Soles of Feet		
Upper Arms		
Elbows		
Forearms		
Wrists		
Hands		
Inner Palms		
Fingers		
Front of Neck		
Whole Face		
Mouth		
Around the Eyes		
Ears		
Front of Skull		
Back of Skull		
Top of the Head		

client
worksheet

Somatic Beliefs of Self

PURPOSE

We have different "bodies." This includes our skeletal, muscular, and fascia body, as well as our emotional, thinking and spiritual body. The way we move, hold our postures, use our muscles and faces can reflect our emotional and thinking life. There is a connection between how we feel and think and how we are; this presents in our bodies. This chart helps you to identify these beliefs and how they show up in the body.

INSTRUCTIONS

Use the body graph to chart the body areas and the beliefs.

- Start with the physical body and note what you are sensing in the body. You can write on the body graph or circle the areas you feel and sense.

- Now focus on the emotional beliefs that stem from the physical experience of the body, such as: "My tense shoulders feel like I am carrying rocks and burdens for my family."

- Move to the thinking body. This is what you believe about the physical and emotional experience. For example, "I carry these rocks because I feel responsible for what happened to my family. It's my fault."

- Pick two to three core beliefs that are most familiar and govern your daily experience. Reflect on these beliefs and look for how your body and your mind are interconnected.

Thinking Body—What do you believe?   **Example:** I have to do it all alone. I can't do enough. It's my fault.

Emotional Body—What do you feel?   **Example:** I feel a heavy burden on my shoulders.

Physical Body—What do you sense and function?   **Example:** Shoulders are tense.

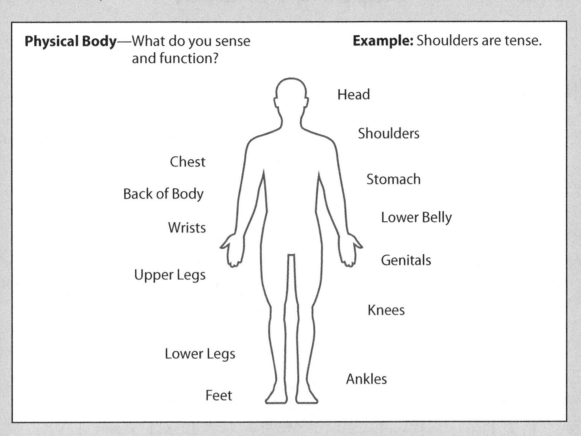

Head

Shoulders

Chest

Stomach

Back of Body

Lower Belly

Wrists

Genitals

Upper Legs

Knees

Lower Legs

Ankles

Feet

My core beliefs are:

1. _____

2. _____

3. _____

Mapping the Body

INSTRUCTIONS

In this quick exercise, you will color or draw on the body any areas of interest. As if you are making a drawing snapshot of your internal landscape, project the inner world in color onto the drawing. Use your imagination and creativity.

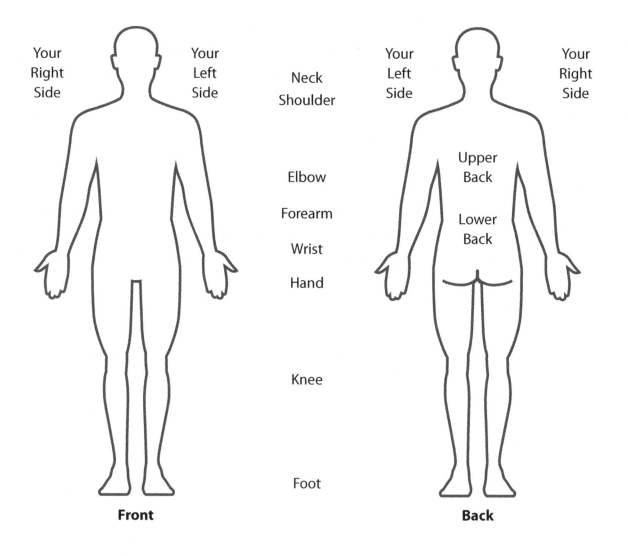

Your Right Side — Your Left Side

Neck
Shoulder

Elbow

Forearm

Wrist

Hand

Knee

Foot

Front

Your Left Side — Your Right Side

Upper Back

Lower Back

Back

therapist worksheet

Body Reading for the Therapist

PURPOSE

- Remember that you are looking through your own filters of perception and biases. Try to be as clear and precise about what you see and what you read and interpret!

- Allow yourself to "see" the person with soft eyes, occasionally doing snapshots as you "read" them.

- Have a sense of what it is like to live in this body. What are the themes this person carries; what do you imagine? How has their unique story shaped the body?

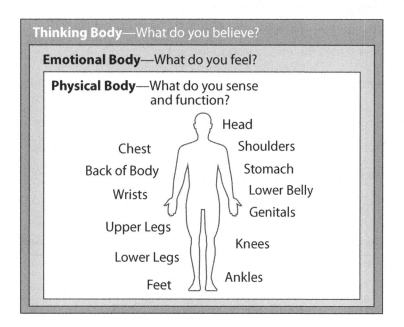

INSTRUCTIONS

- The attitude of this body reading inquiry should be one of compassion, receptivity, curiosity, safety, and playfulness. It's important to view the body with kindness and a perspective of curiosity. Have the information come to you. This is not about judging or categorizing the body, but helping you "see" themes, feelings and shapes in the body that can help you to understand the internal world of the client.

Look at body facts: Take a look at the shape, color, and size of the body without any judgment.

- Size/Height
- Shape (pear, apple, rounded, angular, etc.)
- Color of skin, variability
- Left/Right balance
- Up/Down balance

In a playful attitude consider:

- What part of the body calls your attention and why?
- If you had to assign a bumper sticker, what would it be?
- If there was a kind of wind, what direction would it come from?
- What kind of childhood can you imagine?
- If they were an animal, which one would they be?
- What character in a play do you see?
- What kind of child do you see?
- How do you see the balance of body/mind/spirit mirrored?
- What part of the body seems strongest?
- What parts of the body are hidden?
- What do you imagine is this body's greatest resource?
- Where does their body boundary end?

Assessment:

I see: _____

I imagine: _____

I make up a story about: _____

How does this information help you to "see" the whole person now?_____

_____

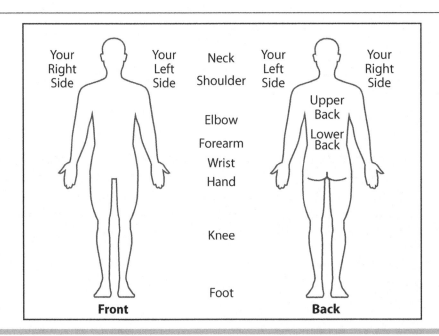

CHAPTER 11

The Somagram and Body Parts

Exploring the body through the techniques of Somagram and Body Parts is a form of mapping the inner experience from the inside-out towards externalization. This process helps you to "see" patterns and experiences we feel and are challenged to put into words. By drawing emotional splits that are felt in the body, we can begin to see them and understand the psycho-emotional divides and can name them more concretely. Make sure you go with the feel and sense of the experience first and then, after you draw and externalize the experience, sit back and reflect on what you see. This will bring much surprising insight and deep understanding and hopefully more compassion to what you experience.

client worksheet

Somagram #1

PURPOSE

Somagram is a visual feedback for the client and therapist. The client draws the sensations and feelings they're experiencing in the body on the provided Somagram. The client is asked to notice what is happening within the body and told how to relate it.

You can perform the Somagram as a daily check-in or as a one-time exercise. The Somagram is a visual aid that helps the client to see how they feel in their body. It also serves as a diagnostic tool for the therapist, to learn what area of the body needs attention.

INSTRUCTIONS

Before beginning, make sure you have markers and pens—use different colors.

1. Have the Somagram outline in front of you; choose a few colors.

2. Take a breath and exhale, slow down your attention.

3. Tune into your body and ask: "How am I feeling in this moment?"

4. Ask yourself: "Where am I feeling my body?"

5. Instinctively (without thinking), draw the areas in your body that are responding. For example, you might shade or circle or draw any symbol or color that you like. Allow yourself to express as accurately as you can what you are experiencing.

6. When you are done, take a moment to review your drawing.

7. Write the first "title" that comes to mind.

8. Debrief with your therapist.

Note to therapist:
Once the exercise is done, take time to debrief with the client. Ask your client about the drawing. Refrain from making interpretive comments—this is a tool for self-discovery, not analysis.

Somagram

FRONT OF BODY

BACK OF BODY

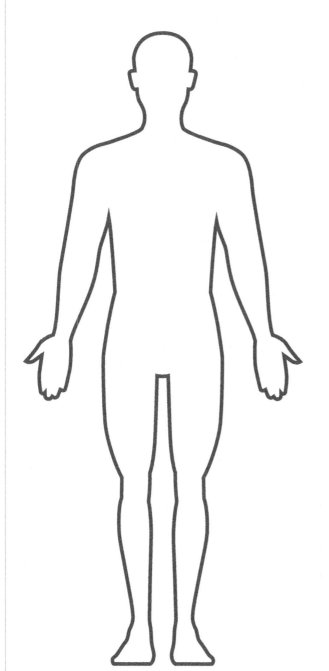

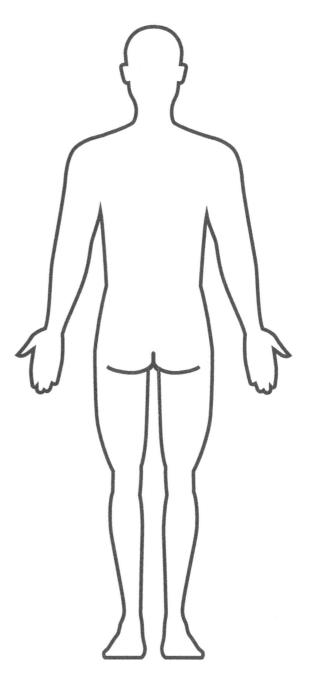

client
worksheet

Somagram #2 - Free Charting

Freely chart your feelings and sensations about your body.

1. How do you feel inside your body?　　**2. How do you see your external body?**

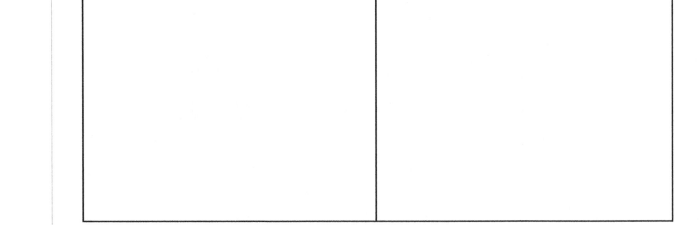

WORKING WITH BODY SPLITS

Body splits are a very common experience in somatic therapy work. Typically, body splits are present when the client makes comments such as: "I can feel one side, but not the other. My left side feels X, the right side Y. I am in touch with my upper body, but numb in my lower body."

There are many variations of body splits: upper body to lower body, right to left side, one body part to another, etc. It is common to have opposing experiences in the inner experience. The key is to become curious and explore these parts in order to discover what is underneath the spilt and what is needed to heal. Try to stay away from interpreting the body splits for the client and allow them to discover what they mean. Body splits can be a temporary experience or a long-standing body pattern. The key is discovery and open curiosity, so the client can find a new meaning.

Working with body splits means:

- Identifying the splits

- Not rejecting the experience, but tuning more into it

- Exploring what one area of the split has to say and the other

- Creating a safe experiment in which the two apparently disparate sides can communicate

- Seeing what wants to happen and trusting that a third new option will emerge

Left/Right Body Split

Chart your experience of the two parts of the body and the spilt.

My Left Side Body is: My Right Side Body is:

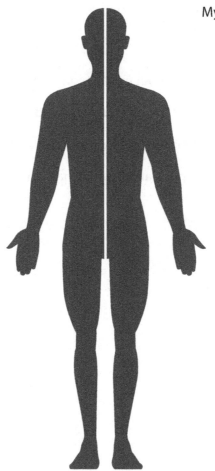

Reflections on my L/R Split:

client
worksheet

Upper/Lower Body Split

Chart your experience of your body and the split

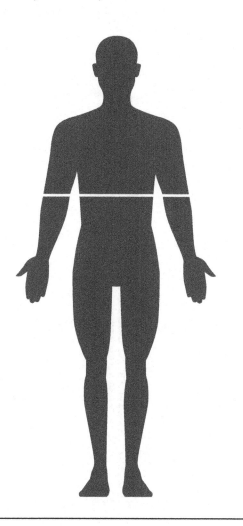

My Upper Body is:

My Lower Body is:

Reflections on my U/L split:

Front/Back Body Split

client
worksheet

Chart your experience of your body. Tune into the front and then the back of the body. Then write down the spilt you experience. Be as specific as you can to discover all the aspects of the split.

My Back of My Body is:

My Front of My Body is:

Reflections on my F/B split:

Body Splits

client worksheet

PURPOSE

Body splits can be experienced throughout the body in different ways. For example, you can feel a split by sensing part of your arm but not your whole arm. Where would you indicate the split? Where is that line between where you feel and sense and where you do not? By mapping out the splits you become aware and can bring your body back into self-awareness.

INSTRUCTIONS

Become quiet and sense your body. Notice what parts of your body feel connected and which ones do not. Notice where the split is.

- List the splits:

    1. _____

    2. _____

    3. _____

    4. _____

Draw your body splits.

- As you tune into where and how you experience the split in your body, you can get information from your body by asking the body about it. Get quiet and tune into what messages or beliefs you associate with the split. Name the belief of the split. If your body split had something to say, what would that be?

_____

_____

- Now think of a positive and nourishing statement for your body. What would the body split want to hear?

_____

_____

- What changes do you notice? As you tune into your body and the splits you identified, how do you view them now?

_____

_____

CHAPTER 12
Presence, Perception and Sensations

Presence, perception and sensations are critical tools to understanding the non-verbal realm of your somatic experiences. How we perceive often determines what we believe and what actions we take. Getting to know the "how" of perception is important to truly grasping deep emotional beliefs and patterns. The more you can open-up and be curious about how your perception works, the more you become present to your direct experience of your body without a filter of inner dialogue or past stories. The self-judgment begins to fade away and you are left with sensing what truly is. There is a truth that emerges when you become present with your body, your sensate experience, and it opens you then to a wider sense of perceiving yourself and the world around you.

To make this simple: The more you can listen to your sensations, the more your perception gets trained to see without bias. Sensations are the raw data.

Start with how you perceive with your eyes. Become aware of how you notice the outer world around you. What do you pay attention to? What attracts your gaze and attention? The more you become present with your perceptions the more it will become a natural next step to become curious about how you perceive from the inside-out. Working with your visual perception leads you towards perceiving your interior world without judgment. The more you can stay present with what is, the more the somatic landscape of your body will "speak" to you. This can be in an actual body awareness, new sensation images, dream images, connecting meaning, having new thoughts or insights, and intuition. It is as if you are learning a new and at the same time familiar language. Asking yourself how you are and what the body is telling you takes some practice. You begin to become with how you perceive your inner and outer experience. Stay present!

client exercise

Soft Vision

PURPOSE

The way we look out of our eyes and see is often very direct, focused and harsh. The eyes strain and get overworked and this can lead to tension headaches and eye strain. Staring at a screen for hours also locks our vision into patterns.

This exercise is about practicing soft vision. We train our vision to de-focus and relax, therefore changing our perception. Soft vision relaxes the tendons of the eye socket.

When perceptions shift, so does the inner perception of how we view the world.

INSTRUCTIONS

- Start by tuning into the awareness of your eyes and vision.

- What do you notice?

- Focus your eyes on an object in the room.

- Now soften the focus as you are looking at the object. Take the focus off and soften the eye socket and the tendons around the eyes. Allow your vision to become soft and a little blurry.

- Close your eyes and rest them. Take a breath, relax.

- Open your eyes and do not focus on anything. See if you can have your eyes not aim for anything. Soften your gaze.

- Tune into your breath and exhale as you keep softening.

- Go until you feel a relaxation, an ease, or a letting-go in your body.

- Now use your eyes and orient around the room, looking gently and with a soft focus.

- What is different?

- What are you perceiving?

Gentle Head Lift

PURPOSE

The head is a heavy part of our body. It weighs between 9-11 pounds for the average person. Headaches, aches and tiredness are common stressors and are felt in the head and neck area. Through the face, head and neck we engage the world. When working with the head, use very small (I mean very small) movements. You want to avoid straining the muscles in the neck.

INSTRUCTIONS

Notice your head in a neutral position. Note any tensions in the head or associated areas, such as neck, jaw and face.

Name the tension:

My head feels_____right now.

- Ever so slowly (as if you are moving at snail speed), and while imagining floating in water or air, lift the head.

- Close your eyes; feel the lifting inside.

- Come back to neutral.

- Now bow the head towards the heart; have your inner gaze look towards the heart.

- Come back to neutral.

- Repeat three times VERY SLOWLY. This is the key element. It's not a stretch or getting out the tension; this is moving the head in a new and light or fluid way.

- Make sure you don't overstretch or add anything. Simply lift-neutral-bow-neutral-repeat.

- Then pause and notice.

Name the change:

My head feels_____ right now.

client exercise

Hands Over Eye Sockets

PURPOSE

This quick and effective five-minute relaxation technique fosters sensations and instills immediate ease in the eye region. You can use this practice when you feel eye strain, a sense of fatigue or a need to tune into your inner world. Covering and resting back into the eyes is an easy way into your inner experience.

INSTRUCTIONS

- Sit down.

- Rest your elbows on your knees.

- Cup the palms of your hands gently over your eye sockets. Make sure you are not pressing into the eye sockets, but cupping them.

- Feel the pressure of the rims of your palms on the rims of your eye sockets.

- Notice the darkness and pressure and take that in.

- Take three deep breaths and exhale with mindfulness.

- What changes?

- What happens when you gently take your hands away? Do you feel more centered or in yourself? What kind of sensations are you aware of?

- What happens to your vision or perception now?

- I notice my eyes being_____

client worksheet

Sensing Your Fluid Brain

PURPOSE

The cerebral spinal fluid (CSF) is found in the nervous system. Characteristics of tuning into the fluid system of our body are associated with meditative states, effortlessness, stillness and a sense of flow in the spine. The CSF is produced in the ventricles of the brain and moves along the spinal cord. It continues through the spinal and cranial nerves and into the fascia and connective tissue of the body into all the cells of the body. The CSF nourishes the entire body by cycling back from the cells through the veins of the heart and lymphatic vessels. The CSF is very slow moving. Think of it as a very slow inner movement that is happening continuously to a different inner rhythm. When you connect with that rhythm, you are slowing down and tuning into subtle levels of your experience. It has a different rhythm than that of the breath and pulse rhythms of the body.

The sutures on your cranium are movable and fluid, not static. Imagine your skull being fluid and supple, not hard.

This exercise can be useful when you experience headaches, stress, tension, or an overactive mind.

INSTRUCTIONS

Draw your brain and head <u>before</u> the exercise. How does it feel to you?

Steps:

- Sit comfortably and quietly.

- Place each of your hands on the sides of your head.

- Give your head a gentle squeeze with each exhale, as if you are gently pushing into your head. With the inhale, release the pressure of the hands squeezing.

- Synchronize the head squeeze with the breath; slow it down with each breath cycle.

- Do five to six slow, focused breaths. Then lower your hands.

- Notice your head and focus your attention now on your cranium. Can you sense your breath in your cranium?

- Make a very, very small movement in your head/cranium. You want to make the movement so small that it is barely visible from the outside. This movement will be initiated in your whole head, but let that movement be felt in the cranium.

- Do about two to three movements, then stop and notice again.

- Can you sense a fluidity inside your body? How does your skull feel?

Draw your brain and head after the exercise. What changes do you notice?

client
exercise

The Spaces In-Between

PURPOSE

This exercise is to enhance proprioception sensibility and connection to the environment. The goal is to study what the inner and outer perceptions of the body are like and if you can come into an equal perception of both.

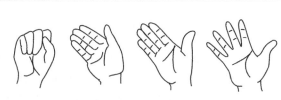

Now relax your hand to check the natural spacing between your fingers!

INSTRUCTION

- Become mindful with your eyes open.
- Look around the room and notice the space in-between objects: Between chair legs, the wall space between paintings, the space between ceiling and floor. See how many spaces in-between objects you can make out just by looking around.
- Now focus on the space in-between your fingers. Look at your hand and notice that there is space between each finger. Start with a closed hand or fingers closed and then gently open the fingers. Start with the thumb and the first finger and so forth. Focus in on the opening and spaciousness between the fingers.
- Close your eyes. Can you still "feel" that space in-between? How is that changing your inner sense of your hand?
- Next, notice the space between thoughts, inner pictures and mental images. Allow the space to be there and rest in the space in-between.

Are you more slowed down? Do you have an awareness of not just the density of your body, but the body in relation to the environment that you are connected to?

Describe how your body feels in relation to the environment right now:

_____

_____

_____

Note to therapist:

You can ask the client to describe the experience. Guide the client to focus on the space in-between. Track for slowing down and more mental spaciousness. The world is more than ideas and concepts.

Dual Awareness

PURPOSE

This exercise will help cultivate simultaneous attention. Dual awareness can be helpful in training your perception and presence. When you can "be with" your body sensation, you train awareness. In dual awareness, you are training yourself to be present with your body, your mind and your feelings. This is effective in work situations or moments of chaos in your life. It can also be very helpful when working with trauma as you can be with your experience while being present to a much broader sense of your environment at the same time.

INSTRUCTIONS

- Become aware of your breath; the sensation of it going in and out of your nostrils.

- Follow the sensation: The rise and fall of your chest, belly engagement, etc. Stay with that for a while until you notice a settling quality.

- Notice the rhythm of your breath.

- Expand your awareness to include the perception of sound, silence, ambient sound, etc. *(Therapist: You can ring a bell or make a sound for the client to notice.*

- Stay with both the awareness of sound and breath/sensation. You can practicing holding a dual awareness now. You notice all at the same time.

- Allow any sensations to arise: Don't dwell; notice and release.

- Collapse all attentions into one: Simply notice.

- Close practice.

client exercise

Bumper Stickers - Reminders for the Body

PURPOSE

These bumper stickers are reminders of the present for your body. For example, when you doubt your body experience, it might be helpful to see the "trust your body wisdom" sticker. You could also stick one on your computer. When you feel tension in your eyes from staring at the computer, you can glance at the sticker and take a break from the screen. Perhaps do the Tool #43: Hands Over Eye Sockets practice. These bumper stickers should serve as a daily reminder to practice coming back home to your body.

INSTRUCTIONS

- Write a series of reminders to yourself using paper, index cards, Post-It® notes, etc. Examples include: "Trust Your Body Wisdom," "Be Kind to Your Body," or "Be Present with Your Body."

- Ask yourself: What reminder does my body need? Get creative.

- Cut these reminders out (if needed).

- Stick them where you will see them, and in places where the reminders will be most helpful.

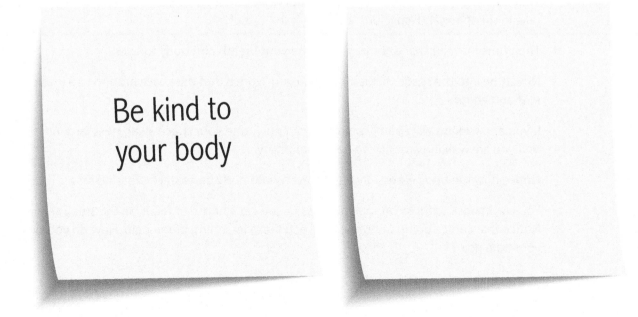

Be kind to your body

Sensing Space

PURPOSE

This exercise is an excellent practice when you want to work with emotional or physical pain. When pain arises in the body, the tendency is to over-focus on it or become tense in the body. There can be a tendency to collapse and feel less spacious. When space collapses, the options to work with oneself decrease. This tool works with "space"—both as a metaphor and quite literally. If you attune to "space" before working with a painful or constricted area in the body, you find your body more willing to open to more sensations, rest or emotional availability.

INSTRUCTIONS

Take between five to 10 minutes to complete.

- Sit comfortably with your eyes open, not focusing on anything, but being aware of your surroundings without grasping your attention.

- Relax your body and mind as much as you can at this moment.

- If there is a painful place in the body, see if you can direct your attention away from it for right now.

- Settle into your breath and body as much as you can.

- Tune into the space in front of you. The trick is for your eyes to be soft, not focused, but still take in the space and "spaciousness" that is in front of you.

- Then tune into the space above you. Settle your breath and body further.

- Now tune into the space that is all around you. Notice that the space around you is open and vast and neutral.

- If you are working with bodily pain, you can now tune your space awareness "around" the pain, as if you are walking around the pain's periphery.

- Notice how the body eases. Pay attention to what body parts start releasing first.

- You can choose to focus on spaciousness or you can choose to focus on the small area of pain. Notice that choice point. Continue until you feel a lessening of the pain. How do you perceive your pain now?

CHAPTER 13
Movement Interventions

MOVEMENT TAKES ALL FORMS

When clients hear the suggestion of doing a movement exploration or exercise, some might freeze and assume they are supposed to dance through the room. Especially when there have been experiences of body shame, stunted expressions or physical trauma, the suggested "movement" instruction can be a challenge. For that reason, it is a good practice to explain that the body is always moving. The body moves functionally through space every minute. The body IS movement, through heartbeat, peristaltic gut motion, synovial fluids in the joints—even breath moves the body. The body moves all the time, even when we are sitting still.

In addition, dancing is a profound healing art that provides a deep somatic experience. In the context of the following tools, we are using movement instead of "dance," so the client can more easily engage with the moving body without being challenged to "dance." Of course, if there is willingness by the client to take the movement practices further, please adapt and deepen. The intent is to offer tools that allow the client to feel and experience the benefit of movement without being triggered into shame or negative experiences.

Emotional patterns in the body—fear, anxiety and depression—restrict the full-functioning movement of the body. A moment of terror freezes the body into stillness and limits any range of motion due to fear of being in danger.

When the frozen qualities of movement take over in the body, the motions the body performs become limited to basic functions and do not permit much expression. We can learn to minimize movement, and with that we are limiting feeling well—a life enriched and basic well-being.

To be able to move fluidly, with free expression, is to become embodied.

When we suggest movement to the client, we want to gently remind them that they are always moving and that they can achieve increased range of motion and well-being by doing the exercises.

Often the first step to movement is to meet the client where they are at—that means in the chair. It also means introducing movement slowly, in small steps, and on the client's terms. This is not about cheerleading the client into any performance or going beyond comfort and ability, but to encourage movement that they actually want to connect with. The other fact is that a frozen, fearful, or highly-limited body pattern can learn, or better "remember," to move again. It is not lost. What is needed is the patience of the therapist to encourage the client to find movement again.

Here a few tips when working with movement:

1. Don't go beyond the comfort level of the client. At the same time, gently invite them to explore and discover. Open-inquiry questions such as "How does this movement want to unfold?" can be helpful.

2. Small movements have a big impact; it is not about how big or expressive the movement is, but how mindful and engaged the client is with their moving body.

3. Mindfulness and awareness are essential in moving; always encourage that.

4. Encourage exploration—what feels right and pleasurable in the movement.

5. Move with your client by mirroring when they move so they don't feel like a fish in a bowl. (To learn more about mirroring, see Tool #54: Mirror, Mirror in this chapter.)

6. Psycho-educate your client that movement is natural and it's not necessarily dancing.

7. Connect movement expirations with meaning. Ask the client what they are experiencing and what their meaning is.

8. Start small and build confidence over time.

9. Track for activation level. If the client gets too overwhelmed or can't be with their experience, stop and re-evaluate.

10. Encourage play!

Unfurling

PURPOSE

This exercise uses awareness of the spine to work with themes of coming out of a shell, shyness, and coming towards something that is unsure. The skill of slowly and gently finding a movement through the spine helps awaken one's awareness of the core and spine. The slow and deliberate movement can add more confidence in facing life's uncertainties.

Picture the image of a fern. The fern in its developmental stages unfurls a very tightly coiled leaf. Slowly it unwraps itself until it expands to the fullness of the leaf. Imagine your body unfurling like a fern leaf.

INSTRUCTIONS

- Start standing or sitting. Don't lean your back against anything. If you're sitting, come to the edge of your seat.

- Keep in mind the theme you are working with, such as feeling tight, afraid to open up, or unsure what it means to be open and vulnerable. Write down your answers on the baseline inquiry on the following page before you start.

- Start with your head bowed down towards your chest. Curl into a ball—imagine being a tightly-wrapped fern leaf.

- Notice your breath in this position.

- Gently find an impulse that wants to open and unfurl.

- Move very slowly! Make the unfurling motion that opens the spine and lifts the head. Savor this slow motion.

- Imagine you are the fern leaf that takes a long time to unwrap its tight coil.

- Go ahead and do this movement again. Make sure not to coil inwards, as if you are closing the fern bud again.

- You can repeat this motion a couple of times. Be careful to go slowly and deliberately and feel the moment of the spine.

- After the movement, rest in the openness or a coiled position (whichever feels more appropriate) and notice what has changed.

- Write down your thoughts and answers to the inquiry questions on the next page.

Baseline - Before the movement

How tight do I feel on a scale of 1-10? _____

What holds me back? _____

What is making me re-coil or shut down? _____

What am I afraid of if I open up?_____

Baseline - After the movement

How am I feeling in my body after the movement? _____

On a scale of 1-10, how willing am I to open to the issue/topic at hand? _____

What do I know about what makes me close down now? _____

What do I notice in my body after the movement? _____

What is my perception now on the topic/theme? _____

Describe the experience with one word: _____

client exercise

Wet Sandbag

PURPOSE

This exercise is geared towards feeling the body's boundaries and re-establishing where the body begins and ends. Gravity connects a sense of grounding and belonging. Encourage slowness in movement and awareness of breath. The whole body has contact with the ground, which will provide a sense of connection between body and earth. This is an excellent exercise to do with kids or adults wanting to explore safety and their body's boundaries.

INSTRUCTIONS

This is a body-roll exercise, so you will need floor space. Place a blanket or mat on the floor for comfort.

Note to therapist:

Guide the client to roll like a "wet sandbag," shifting the weight of their body to imitate the shifting movement of wet sand. It is important to move slowly to feel and sense the weight shifting.

What to watch out for:

If a client gets dizzy or uncomfortable, stop and ask them to pay attention to their body. You do not want to disorient the client, but rather tune them in to their sense of body gravity and feeling grounded. The slower they perform the exercise, the more present they can be with their body.

Steps:

- Lay down on one side. Take note of your body against the ground; feel the support. Take a moment to connect with the ground beneath you.
- Allow your body to shift slightly and observe the gravitational pull that is guiding the movement.
- Visualize that you are a wet sandbag rolling on the floor. Very slowly, shift the sand in the bag to initiate the movement. Imagine each grain of sand shifting as gravity pulls it in the next direction; your body simply follows the pull of gravity.
- Notice how the weight rolls you on your back. Allow yourself to rest a moment, and then initiate the next shifting of the sand's weight onto your other side.
- Don't force the movement, but let the shifting, wet sand do the work.
- Keep rolling from one side to another as long as you feel motivated and comfortable.
- When done, slowly sit up and make note of how your body feels.
- Do you feel connected? Do you have a sense of where your body is in relation to the floor and the space around you?
- What awareness of your body did this exercise elicit?

client exercise

Micro-Movement in Neck

PURPOSE

Micro-movements are a category of movements that are easy to do. They are internal, barely visible on the outside. They are internally driven and felt, and can have a big impact on your nervous system. The smaller the movement, the more attentive you are to that small movement, and the more you will sense and feel it in your body.

Therapeutic focus:

1. Calming the nervous system by bringing micro-movements into a small, manageable region of the body.

2. Using micro-movements to work on neck and headache tension.

3. Teaching micro-movements to the client as a resource.

4. Bringing the focus away from the tense area in the neck and releasing it.

INSTRUCTIONS

Guided imagery:

Imagine you are standing in the shower and you have a fogged shower glass in front of you. You gently press the tip of your nose against the glass and start making small circles with the tip of your nose on the glass. Let that movement be so tiny and without effort. Do this several times, then change the direction. You can also do a figure eight. It is important to make this movement fluid and continuous, and without thinking. It is also important to keep the range of movement small so you do not use big muscles in the neck.

Movement focus:

After a while, notice how you are moving the back of your neck. The movement is in the first vertebrae and creates a fluid sense with the neck; it creates this fluidity by not focusing on it. By allowing the neck to move without tension, the neck is able to release. This is a very effective tool for headaches and tensions in the neck and the base of the neck. Make sure to keep the focus on the front of the nose and with the image. Once you become more relaxed, you can move the attention to the neck movement itself.

client exercise

Opening the Horizon

PURPOSE

This exercise synchronizes your breath and movement. Connecting with the horizon is a practice that will center and ground your stress. We have a tendency to become narrow focused when stressed, and opening to the wider horizon is a way to enlarge the "small worldview" we can get stuck in.

This is a wonderful tool to use when time is limited for a longer somatic practice. This can be done anytime, even when you only have five minutes.

INSTRUCTIONS

- Stand up; notice your feet on the floor. Take a firm stand. Relax your upper body.

- Start by looking at the floor, your arms at your sides.

- As you inhale, lift your gaze and follow the gaze with your arm movement so that your eyes, arm movement, and breath are in synch. Keep your hands face up as you inhale.

- Now exhale and bring your gaze downward towards the floor; bring your arm movement downward as well, so your gaze, arm movement, and breath are in synch. As you exhale, keep your hands facing downward, as if you are pressing an imaginary air bubble.

- Repeat this a few times. Keep your movements slow and mindful so your gaze, breath, hand and arm movements are in synch with each inhale and exhale.

- Notice what happens inside your mind and body as you pause.

- When my horizon opens I see_____, I feel_____, I perceive myself to be_____.

client exercise

Walking with Aim

PURPOSE

This exercise regulates the emotional and physiological activation of the client. By walking with an aim, you are matching the inner and outer world of the client.

Therapeutic focus:

This exercise is about giving the client control and focus. The movement of walking engages the gross motor movement and larger muscles of the body, and brings coordination to these movements. It's an orientation with the whole body. Make sure you are matching the pace that reflects the inner activation/feelings of the client. (For example, use a fast walk to match inner anxiety or feelings of being out of control.) For some clients, this starts fast and slows down as they notice calming down. Some clients start slow and then go faster. Experiment with what is right for the client in the moment.

INSTRUCTIONS

Note to therapist:

During this exercise, you may want to walk with the client and match their pace. This will encourage the client and lessen their self-consciousness. Walking is done inside the office if space permits. Taking the client outside the therapy room will require a professional disclosure statement. Walking within the room does not need to take up a lot of space; pacing back and forth in a small area can do the trick.

Steps:
- Pick a focus in the room, any object you like. Walk towards it.
- Once you reach the first object, pick another object and walk to it.
- Keep repeating this.
- Notice how your focus and the walking bring your body in to one coherent and single-focused attention.
- Notice the speed you need. For example, you might have to pick up the speed if you notice any anxiety inside; match the pace until you feel more in control.
- Pause and reflect on the changes that happened.

When I walk with aim I am....

client exercise

Mirror, Mirror

PURPOSE

This exercise emphasizes being seen in one's relationships. By mirroring the client's movement, they can explore what it feels to be seen and witnessed. Mirroring is a basic movement that every mother/ child dyad does and leaves the internal sense of being understood. Mirroring also evokes a sense of play and connection. Be mindful of self-consciousness, you want to ask what is happening and slow down the experience for the client to feel what is arising.

INSTRUCTIONS

This can be done sitting or standing. It's easiest to introduce mirroring movement though the hands first.

- Stand or sit across from each other.

- Slow down your breath and attention.

- Ask your client, "Notice the quality of our connection. On a scale from one to 10, how connected are we right now?"

- Allow the client to mindfully tune into their hands.

- Have them bring their hands up and begin a movement that feels comfortable, starting with a movement that expresses where they're at right now.

- Let their hands slowly move, so the client can be with the movement.

- As the therapist, match the movements exactly, as if the client is standing in front of a mirror.

- Let the client take the lead first, while you follow the movement as closely as possible.

- Now take the lead and ask the client to follow your movement: "Imagine you are standing in front of a mirror and you are following my movements exactly the way I am doing them."

- As the therapist, you can bring a small variation into the movements for some playfulness.

- Only lead for a short while, as the focus is on the client to be seen.

- Switch back to the client leading for another moment.

- Then pause and rest your hands.

- Ask your client for reflection: "Notice your hands; notice the quality of our connection right now. What is your experience at this moment? On a scale from one to 10, what is the level of our connection? What is happening in your body right now as you feel connected?"

client
exercise

Movement Play and Beliefs

PURPOSE

This exercise helps a client playfully explore a body boundary using movement.

INSTRUCTIONS

- Stand or sit across from each other. Hold up your hands and arms as if you were saying "hi."
- One of you make a small movement.
- The other copy that exact movement.
- Go back and forth and copy each other's movements.
- Now one of you make a small variation and wait.
- Notice how the change affects you.
- Let play happen; continue and notice your experience.
- Track for what is happening in your quality of connection.
- Talk with each other about the experience.

Consider these questions:

- What is play?
- What was fun about this exploration?
- What was uncomfortable?
- What do you believe about play?
- When was it too close?
- When was it too far?
- When was it just right?
- What did the play open up in you?

Reflection:

What beliefs do I carry around play?

_____

_____

_____

Figure 8 Resource Movement

PURPOSE

This movement is a bi-lateral and even movement that engages the client's awareness. It calms and soothes activation, and can also serve as an integrative movement after a piece of process. This is a rhythmic and repetitive movement; it's a modulating movement that has integrative functions.

INSTRUCTIONS

- Get into a comfortable standing position; connect with your feet and the ground.

- Close your eyes.

- Imagine your sitting bones having paintbrushes, and as if they want to paint a figure eight on the ground. Follow the gentle movement of a figure eight, letting the hips move slowly at first and finding a rhythm that feels soothing to you. You can play with smaller, larger, slower and faster movements, but then settle into a rhythm and stay with that rhythm.

- Notice how your breath gets involved, especially any exhalations.

- Do this movement for five minutes. Then slowly bring the movement to a smaller and smaller range, until the outer movement stops.

- Although you've stopped, notice how the figure eight continues internally. Track for the sensations inside. Notice any feelings of calm, well-being.

Tips for the therapist:

- If clients get disoriented with this move, ask them to stop moving, open their eyes, and orient in the room. Then, ask them what their relationship with the ground is.

- Avoid clients doing any head swinging—this adds to disorientation. The figure eight stays on the same plane—only the hips move; the shoulders and head ride the movement and are not actively engaged. To stabilize the movement, the client can have their hands resting on their belly.

Defending Arms

PURPOSE

This tool is helpful in establishing a safe body boundary, as well as the expression of saying "no" with a powerful gesture. Using your arms to defend is an instinctive movement that can be used consciously to feel the "no" that the mind wants to express.

INSTRUCTIONS

Note to therapist:

- Teach clients these sequences of arm defenses, instructing them to "rehearse" these possibilities, and coaching them to remember these movements as intrinsic, instinctual and necessary.

- When you observe impulses involving the arms such as pushing, or a split-second halting motion of the hands, have the client slow down and connect with these impulses. Notice where they stop and get stuck, and gently talk them through completing the movement.

- It is important to work slowly and repeat the instructions. Have the client follow the movements. Track carefully when the client becomes dissociative or collapses—they need to pause and resource at that moment.

Track for:

- Sequence of the movement: Is there a beginning, middle and end?

- Any time you observe a client giving up, collapsing, becoming stuck or exhibiting repetitive movement, slow down immediately or interrupt and resource.

- The whole body supporting the movement.

- Images, memories flooding in, or feelings of being overwhelmed. Remember, it is important to move slowly.

- When fast movement is needed; have the client rest frequently and observe for elevated heart rate, which needs to be felt, but not overwhelm.

Defending Sequence:

1. Use the "Halt" position of your hands to signal a "no" or "stop."

2. Have your arms stretched out as if to brace against something or to push someone away.

3. Notice if you feel strength or power in your body. See if you can maintain that body feeling. What can support this?

4. If you had a word to express this posture, what would that be?

Protecting Sequence:

1. Cross your arms in front of your face as your body leans away. It's another way to say "no" or set a boundary.

2. Tune into the protective quality that your arms are giving you.

3. You can protect your body.

4. What words could go with this body stance?

Action Sequence:

1. Push your hands, palm-to-palm, against each another. This will help you feel the strength of your own hands.

2. Imagine pushing your hands against a person who you want to say "no" to or set some kind of boundary with. You can use a repetitive movement, stretching the arms outward, or hold the position of your arms stretched out.

3. Notice how you can support this strong movement with the rest of your body. Do you have your legs firmly under the rest of your body?

4. Let this movement be dynamic and active. Push the arms forward and notice how YOU are making the action happen.

5. Notice your breath. It's not uncommon to feel a faster breath rhythm.

6. Stay mindful of this movement so you stay connected with the action of the movement. Take little breaks and sense into the change of your body.

7. What do you notice?

8. When you feel you've had enough or it's done, take a break and sense into your body.

9. What does the body have to say now?

Orienting Movements

PURPOSE

Orienting movement helps the client to feel safe and in control. You can use this movement any time your client feels anxious or insecure, as well as during the trauma recovery part of the therapy work. It is a basic resourcing and safety-building movement.

This movement reconnects truncated impulses that were threatened and re-establishes the somatic sense of safety. Orienting is natural and we do this movement the moment we are born. However, it can get stuck when one is fearful or anxious. The trick is to liberate these impulses, which can help break through the stuck and anxious places in the body. Track where the client is stuck, or where they become activated. It is very important to go very slowly and deliberately.

As the therapist, you can keep talking to the client while they experience the movement, making sure there are no signs of anxiety or fear. Back up if there are. Only stay in the zone of comfort and control. Encourage the completion of the movement when safety and curiosity are aligned.

INSTRUCTIONS

Guide the client through the sequence of turning away and back again very slowly and mindfully. The orienting movement is a simple head turning, as if you are looking toward the side of your body and towards a point in the room. This should be done very slowly and deliberately so you can sense the turning and how the eyes orient in the room.

Before beginning the exercise, have the client complete the following statement:

"When I am disoriented, my body is: _____."

First Sequence - turning away:

This can be turning away from the therapist as a source or where their eye gaze starts from.

- Let your eyes start by notice what they are seeing.

- Move your eyes away sideways, as if you want to lead the gaze towards one side. You can go left or right; it does not matter.

- Very mindfully scan the room. Imagine your eyes being a searchlight, shining it's light through the space.

- Allow your head to follow the movement of your eyes towards the direction of the shoulder.

- As you continue your eye movement towards the side of the body, let your neck and shoulders follow the head movement.

- There will be a slight trunk rotation as you complete the motion.

- When you can't turn any farther, rest your gaze on one point in the room. Allow yourself to really look at an object in the room.

- Then slowly return the head towards the middle of the body. This starts the second sequence.

Second Sequence - turning back:

- Reverse the first sequence.

- Start with the slightly-rotated trunk returning towards the middle of the body. Let the shoulders follow, and then the head.

- The eyes should be naturally following this body motion, as if they are slowly scanning the room.

- In this sequence, the eyes are reversing the pathway back toward the middle of the body, towards the starting point of the gaze.

Working with the sequence:

Notice if the movement and the sequence itself becomes un-sequential. For example, the head might turn very fast without any awareness. Have the client slow it down, go back and repeat. Talk them through this out loud: "Notice your trunk turning, then the shoulders following, then the head. Notice how your eyes want to come back to my face; and notice this as one complete movement."

Or you might notice that the motion is not very fluid. Ask the client to slow down and take a breath. See if they can relax a little.

Perhaps you track a vigilance in the eyes, a quick flittering gaze that can't be steady. You might name this and ask them to scan the room more calmly and steadily by keeping the eyes on one plane rather than searching around the room.

When in doubt, slow the movement down so the client can notice what is happening. The point is to introduce a tool where the client can create a safety zone by learning how to orient.

The client will have to repeat the sequence often, until they have the sequence of the movement—breaks in the sequence are indicative of emotions or sensations not being processed.

Scanning for safety:

After the orienting sequence, have the client scan the room. If they want to do the sequence again, have them do it. Notice how there is less activation and more control.

Following the exercise, have the client complete the following worksheet:

Orienting Movements

Chart your experience of your body. Tune into the front and then the back.

"When I am oriented my body is: _____."

Circle the somatic markers in your body when you know you are oriented in time and space.

Spacious	Strong Legs	Feet Awareness	Belly Connected
Wide	Strong Gaze	Shoulder Awareness	Earth Connected
Clear	Power	Heart Awareness	Feeling My Face
No Fear	Fierce	Chest Awareness	Knowing Where I Am
No Anxiety	Calm	Grounded	Now: Present Moment

Your own description:

CHAPTER 14
Boundaries

THE IMPORTANCE OF SETTING BOUNDARIES

Setting boundaries is an essential skill. Before we can set boundaries, we need to "feel and sense" our boundaries. Those who grow up in families with poor boundaries or have had their boundaries invaded often experience traumatic boundary breaches. Boundary work is an essential aspect of healing one's sense of personal safety and space.

The purpose of this next section is to somatically experience what it is like to have a boundary respected and notice it in one's own body.

When you use the boundary exercises, make sure that you proceed with care and go slowly enough so the client can notice any change or discomfort. If the client notices a discomfort, pause and have them inquire. When in doubt back up, pause, and make sure the client is in "control" of the exercise. Since boundary work has often had a violation preceding it, make sure you are extra mindful.

The purpose of these exercises is to "empower" your client to first feel, then assert, their boundaries. Track for the tendency to withdraw or minimize when learning how to set boundaries.

Below are some inquiry questions you can play with when working with boundaries. You can ask them to yourself to assess your client's sense of boundaries or whenever it seems appropriate.

General inquiry questions:

- Where does the other person begin, and where do I start?

- Where are we in relation to one another?

- When do I know you are too close?

- What tells me you are too far away?

- What part of me wishes you were farther away?

- What part of me wishes you were closer?

client exercise

Body Boundary

PURPOSE

Body boundaries begin with the sense of our own personal space. This exercise can be used when the client has difficulty sensing their own personal space, or if they feel a lack of boundaries. Working with one's own physical muscles can re-establish the internally-felt boundary. Here we use the awareness of muscle contraction to sense a body boundary.

INSTRUCTIONS

Work with contracting and releasing muscles in your body. This activity will let you sense into your body as a boundary. Make sure you go slowly and deliberately. At first, you want to feel the body boundary as you contract and then feel the lack of it when you release.

- Start with a muscle that feels easy to access, such as your hand or arm. With your muscle, flex and tense and slowly release. Track the response in your body.

- Then move to the belly (core) and tense the muscle and slowly release. Make sure you are not releasing fast, but with control and awareness so you can track what is occurring in the release.

- Track the sensations that come along with this contracting movement. Allow yourself to be with the sensations.

- Tense and flex any other muscles you like and experiment.

- Report to the therapist as you do this. The focus is on having a sense of body awareness and control without overwhelm.

- After you contract-release for a while, can you notice how your body boundary stays even if you release? How do you experience that?

Note to therapist:

Pace your client through this. You can take frequent pauses, having them close their eyes, before proceeding with another round. Don't overdo it. If you do this too many times, the sensations might dull. Have them contract-release three times, then pause and reflect and report to you. You are looking for a sense of strength, boundary, and empowerment.

client exercise

Extending a Physical Boundary

PURPOSE

This is a good follow-up exercise after you have experienced your body boundary. Practice the body boundary exercise first before engaging with this one.

INSTRUCTIONS

This exercise brings the boundary awareness into a relationship. As the therapist, make sure you are comfortable being the exercise partner here. The focus is for the client to feel their boundary in a relationship, so they can measure if they feel strong in asserting their boundary or not.

- Become aware of your own body boundary by either imagining or drawing an imaginary circle around your body. You can also briefly do the contract-release technique to sense into your boundary.

- Notice the other person/therapist sitting opposite you. What is that like? Can you feel your boundary as you take in their presence? If not, see if you can re-draw your imaginary or physical boundary.

- Can you assert your boundary? If not, what is happening? If yes, what else do you need to make that boundary stronger?

- Are there any words or statements that go with this experience?

- Play with a menu of setting a physical boundary by keeping in mind that you are doing this toward someone.

Note to therapist:

If your client is having a challenging time asserting their boundary in relationships, you can try these additional experiments:

1. Stretch your arm out (client or therapist)

2. Stretch arm and turn head

3. Say "no" or "stop" with arm gesture

4. Experiment with both arms towards the person

5. Move away slightly with chair

6. Come up with your own favorite combo

client
exercise

Muscle Tone Boundary

PURPOSE

This exercise should be used when the client feels without boundaries or unprotected.

The focus is to have the client experience a sense of body awareness and control without being overwhelmed. Take a baseline before the exercise to study the effect of the exercise so you can compare the beginning and end results. The goal is to help the client gain control of their body and responses. Go slowly and systematically.

INSTRUCTIONS

Baseline before the exercise:

My body boundary feels _____.

I can sense my boundary when I _____ around myself.

I can sense tightness in this area of my body: _____.

I can sense numbness or nothing in this area of my body: _____.

Steps:

• Start with a muscle that feels easy to access, such as hands. Flex and tense the hands into a fist and slowly release. Repeat one to two times. Notice the sensations in the hands.

• Now flex and tense the arm muscle by slowly curling the biceps—as if you are lifting an imaginary weight—and slowly release. Repeat one to two times. Notice the response in your body.

• Now move to the belly and tense it by pulling in the core muscle of the belly towards the belly button. Gently exhale as you contract. Then slowly release. Make sure you are not releasing fast, but with control and awareness so you can track what is occurring in the release. Repeat one to two times.

• Next tense the gluteus muscle in the buttocks as if you are lifting up your seat. Contract and release gently and with control. Repeat one to two times. Notice the sensations as you release.

• Now contract and release the leg muscles by turning them towards each other. Track the sensation; see if you can be with them. Repeat one to two times. Notice if it is easier for you to contract or relax.

• Now move to the feet; curl the toes and release. Repeat one to two times.

- Tense and flex any other muscles you like one to two times. Make sure you focus on the release and don't remain tensed.

- When you are done, relax the body. Close your eyes and stay with the sensations of the body. Study the inner experience right now.

- Can you sense your body more? Can you feel where your body boundary is? How do you sense the outer border of your body right now?

Baseline after the exercise:

Now my body boundary feels_____.

I can sense my boundary when I _____ around myself.

Revisiting the tightness I had before the exercise, I can now feel: _____.

Revisiting the numb areas of my body, I can now feel: _____.

client
exercise

Wrapping Yourself into Your Own Space

PURPOSE

This exercise facilitates the client's ability to feel their physical body boundaries on a sensorial level. As babies, for example, the comfort of a blanket or wrap helped us to somatically feel our body boundary. This exercise is particularly helpful when the client feels the need to be held, wrapped, or protected.

What you will need:

A light blanket or shawl long enough to wrap around the client's shoulders and body. Tip: Use a sari made from a robust material, as it's longer and wraps nicely around the body.

INSTRUCTIONS

Use this technique when the client wants to feel protected, a sense of safety, or is feeling withdrawn. You can either wrap the shawl around the client or hand it to them to wrap. Assess for their comfort level. Ask if they want you to wrap them; don't assume.

- Have the ends of the shawl in your hand and gently twist the ends, that way you can apply gentle pressure on the wrapping motion.
- Explain what you will be doing so they can relax and enjoy the comfort of the wrapping.
- Wrap over the shoulders or the midsection of the belly. Please avoid the head!
- Gently hold the ends and turn them like a tourniquet so pressure applies on the wrap.
- Imagine that the shawl is an extension of your touch, so use caution and go slowly.
- Notice when the client wants to come out of it and slowly release the pressure and let go of the shawl.
- Debrief with them how their body feels now AFTER they had the wrap on their body.
- Can they feel their body boundary now?

Script:

"I am wrapping your shoulders right now and I'll be holding the ends of the shawl to apply some gentle pressure. This is so you can feel the wrapping on your skin.

I am going very slowly, so you can tell me when it feels ideal and comfortable to you. When you feel the pressure matches what you need inside, tell me and we will pause there.

Now allow yourself to feel this protective boundary. Notice what happens when you feel that.

When you are ready, I will slowly release the pressure. Notice what that is like."

After the wrap is off: "Notice what your body feels like now. Can you sense a body boundary?"

Personal Space Exploration

INSTRUCTIONS

The box below is a relationship you are in. Where do you position yourself in relation to the other person? Draw your ideal distance.

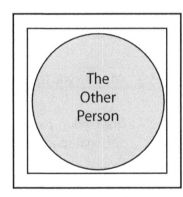

Follow-up questions:

What would you need to set this boundary? _____

What stands in the way of setting this boundary? _____

What can help you learn how to set this boundary? _____

client
worksheet

Boundary Homework for Personal Space

PURPOSE

Boundaries help define your personal space. Boundaries can be physical, emotional, verbal, behavioral and spiritual. They can also be strong, rigid, loose, open, flexible, distant, close, merged, or fluid. There are internal boundaries and also external boundaries between you and other people. This exercise will help you reflect on your boundaries.

INSTRUCTIONS

Use the following questions to help you assess your boundaries.

Inquiry questions:

- How would you describe your personal boundaries?

- How can you tell where your personal space begins and ends?

- What do you feel in your body when someone comes too close to your personal space?

- What do you feel in your body when someone is too far from your personal space?

- Draw your personal space. Make a circle around the figure to indicate your personal space.

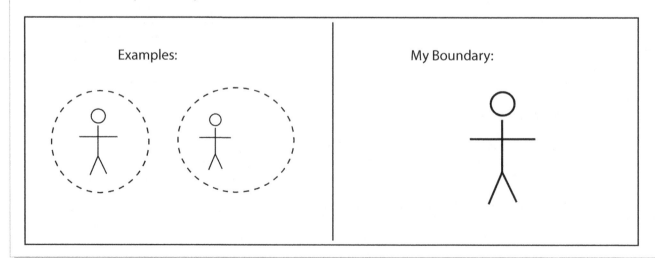

- What color would your boundary be? _____

- What material would your boundary be made of? _____

- Who is in your personal space and who is not?

Examples:

Friends

Close Friends

Acquaintances

Family

New People

Extended Family

Partner

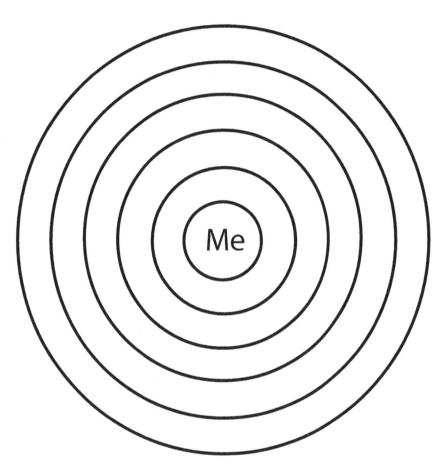

- What kind of boundaries did your family have? Were they strong, rigid, loose, open, flexible, distant, close, merged, fluid, etc.?

- Who in the family had the rigid boundaries and who had the loose boundaries?

- Think of a time when you did not feel comfortable and someone was too close to you. Imagine drawing a boundary around you as you envision this scenario. What words or actions can you take to re-establish this boundary?

client worksheet

When Boundary is Violated - Re-drawing the Territory

PURPOSE

This exercise is designed to re-draw physical and emotional boundaries when your boundaries have been violated. The therapist can guide you through this visualization or you can visualize it by yourself.

INSTRUCTIONS

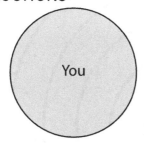

You

Visualize yourself and your personal body boundary. What do you need to feel safe?

1. _____

2. _____

3. _____

4. _____

5. _____

6. _____

7. _____

8. _____

9. _____

10. _____

The Other Person

Visualize the "other" person that you want to set a boundary with. What can you say to them in order to state your boundary?

1. _____

2. _____

3. _____

4. _____

5. _____

6. _____

7. _____

8. _____

9. _____

10. _____

Make a statement that will affirm your motivation to set and state your boundaries. Write down the most essential boundary that you are working on. Post this declaration and notice what changes inside as you do so.

I need _____boundary.

I need you to respect my boundary by _____.

I am asking you to consider my boundary request by_____.

I will no longer_____.

Personal Space in Relation

PURPOSE

This exercise brings awareness to your body boundary in relation to how you position yourself to another.

INSTRUCTIONS

- Start by visualizing a person whom you have an easy time with and imagine sitting across from them. How close or far would you sit from them? What is the optimum distance? How do you know that this is the optimum space between you?

- Now imagine a person you have a more difficult time with. Where is the optimum space between you? Is it easy to set that boundary? Difficult? What makes it difficult? What is in the way?

- Draw your ideal relationship distance. The box is the relationship you are in. Where do you position yourself in relation to the other person?

What would you need to set this boundary?

_____

What stands in the way of setting the boundary?

_____

What can help you in learning to set the boundary?

_____

Take a look at the drawing; sense into this new boundary you just set. What do you notice in your body? What words go with the experience you are having right now?

_____

_____

_____

Journal about the boundaries you know have been invaded and not treated with respect. Write down some key moments that you remember. What do these key moments have in common?

_____

_____

_____

_____

_____

_____

_____

Write down ONE aspect you can change regarding your boundary setting. A word? A sentence you want to say to yourself inside? A feeling in the body you want to remember and come back to?

Remember, learning to set boundaries starts with a clear and concise statement of what you are not willing to do or be anymore.

I will change my boundaries by saying/doing: _____.

Take a stand for my boundary with this statement:

_____

_____

_____

String Exercise in Relationship

PURPOSE

This exercise guides the client into finding their own personal space and becoming aware of how to set boundaries. The exploration involves experimenting with how to feel into a boundary and know when a boundary needs to be set. This exercise can be adjusted to fit the client's need and exploration. It is important that this exercise is done mindfully so that the client has time to somatically feel where the boundary is and is not.

What you will need:

You will need two strings long enough to make a large circle around each body.

INSTRUCTIONS

This is a partner exercise and is done in relationship to the therapist. It's also an excellent group activity done in pairs.

Set up:

- Instruct the client that this exercise is done best on the floor. Assess for their comfort level to move to the floor. If needed you can adjust to doing this exercise in chairs.

- Have the strings ready, one for the client and one for the therapist.

- Orient the client that this exercise is an exploration of boundaries. Discovering where the absence of boundaries exists is important in order to explore where and how boundaries need to be established.

Therapist's instructions:

- Make sure you instruct the client and explain the exercise before you launch into it.

- Be mindful and slow down.

- It's an exploration, so you want to be open to the client's input and creativity.

- Encourage the client with open-ended questions (included in the "Script" section that follows).

- The goal is to discover how the boundaries are felt internally and learn how to create boundaries with the help of visually setting boundaries.

- Sit facing each other.

- Allow some time after the exercise to discuss the experience. Make sure that each time you are asking for an adjustment, you notice what that is like for the client and help them notice their body. You want the client to feel empowered and safe as they are doing the exercise.

Script:

- Take a moment and settle down in a seated position on the floor with your string near you.

- Allow yourself to slow down and become mindful.

- Feel into your body and notice what it is like to have me sit across from you.

- Notice where your body boundary is at this time.

- Notice where your personal space is right now.

- Mark your personal space with the string.
    - Is it close to your body?
    - Is it far from your body?
    - Does the string go all the way around?

- When you have marked your personal space, notice what it is like when I am marking my space.
    - What is that like for you?
    - Is it too close? Too far?
    - How do you know?

- Notice what kind of adjustments you need to make after you see my boundary.

- Go ahead and adjust your string if needed.
    - Do you need to make your space bigger, smaller?
    - Do you need to re-draw that boundary?

- If you have the "right" distance, notice how that feels in your body.

- What do you need to do to feel safer or more comfortable?

- Slowly move within your circle and see what it's like to relate to me from within the string bubble.

- Next, while I am slowly moving around inside my string bubble, notice what that is like for you.

- Pause and notice again what is happening to our relationship as we are adjusting and setting boundaries.

- Next, come to the middle and adjust one more time to what feels like the right boundary between us.

- Make a statement if you wish of what this feels like.

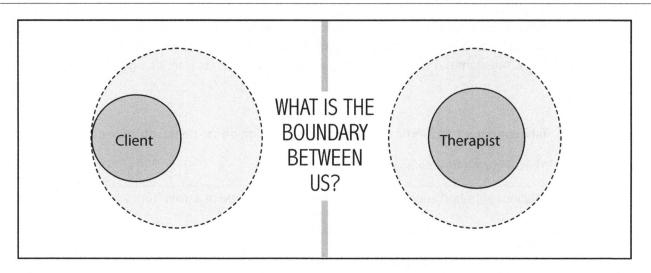

Questions to facilitate the exploration:

- What is the boundary between us?

- How do you know this boundary?

- What tells you that there is a boundary?

- How do you feel/sense it?

CHAPTER 15
Posture

POSTURE AND INTERNAL MESSAGES

Posture reflects the inner climate of a person. We carry unconscious beliefs about our bodies as well as messages we have received on how our body looks.

Messages such as "sit up straight," "shoulders back," "you look too tall, too short, too big, too small" are often given in subtle communications. Self-consciousness while growing into the pubescent body can affect the physical posture for a lifetime. A lack of "feeling good in the body" can result in chronic body posture patterns that lock the person in an internal body state.

Posture is a direct way we can "read" the body's internal state as a therapist; it also offers direct ways of working with the client's mood and feelings.

Start by gently identifying the messages the person has received about their posture. How do they feel about themselves standing, sitting or being observed from the outside by others? What internalized messages does the client carry about their body posture, its movement and function?

Standing up straight actually defeats the purpose, as a straight spine is not anatomically correct. The natural spine is curved and the alignment of the spine with the rest of the body is what we want to consider "straight." Straight actually means an inner and outer alignment of the body with a sense of well-being. Clients often don't even know what that means until they experiment from the inside-out, rather than how the body is seen by others or self-judged.

Chronic fear shapes the body from the inside-out. Reflexes and strong feelings that are not resolved bring mechanical changes to the body structure. Muscle tensions that are ignored begin to shape the client's inner experience and reactivity. Posture can be the first gateway into the sense of how the body's feelings, emotions and muscular responses are in a dynamic interplay and interconnected. Kinesthetic sensations are connected with the central nervous system through bones, joints and fluids, and together inform the proprioceptive sensibilities and perceptions.

Simple actions such as walking, sitting and standing can provide an excellent way to enter the body's posture without the client needing to "do movement." The aspect of "meeting the client where they are at" in their basic movement functions can bring body awareness and somatic readiness to a wide range of clients.

Having the client tune into their basic sense of gravity and movement can open up new perceptions of how they experience themselves from the inside. A lumbering walk with mindfulness can point the client to their sense of emotional heaviness, which is expressed in their walk. Ask them a simple question such as: "What could you change right now as you walk this way?" This open inquiry brings an awareness and pathway that they can change right now.

The Lengthy Spine

PURPOSE

Posture is fundamental to a person's well-being, in addition to expressing one's internal world. For example, a collapsed chest that curves inward combined with downcast eyes indicates a sad or frightened posture. First, we want to understand:

1. What created the posture in the first place?

2. What can we do "now" from the inside-out to change the posture, bringing along the emotions that are connected to the body?

Note to therapist:

Resist telling your client to change their posture to how you want it, or what you think is best. Have them discover the necessary resources and pathways internally to make that shift. You are teaching them the *process* of posture change, not the end result.

Use this technique when you are noticing, or the client complains of, their posture being collapsed, compressed or out of alignment. This exercise serves to find the healthy alignment of a lengthy spine that reflects a sense of well-being and connection with the body. This is a good technique to use when the client feels deflated, slightly dissociated, or complains of compression in the posture.

INSTRUCTIONS

This exercise is done standing. Ask your client to stand up. (This exercise can be modified to a sitting position if needed.) Make sure you track how the posture is initially and what emotions and sensations accompany the posture. Allow some time to explore the posture to find the meaning in this. Clients often take posture as a given and don't realize that their emotional life is very connected with how they are inhabiting their posture.

- Notice your posture right now. Tune into your spine and become aware of what is. Don't make any changes yet; just notice what is.

- Allow your attention to be inward with your posture. As if you had eyes on the inside of your spine, allow yourself to look into your posture. Are your shoulders forward or back? Is your chest open or collapsed? Are your hips aligned with your shoulders? Are your feet connected with your legs? Your legs underneath your pelvis? Is your pelvis forward or back? What feels in and out of alignment? Verbalize as you experience what you are sensing from your posture internally.

- Make a comment on how this posture feels. Is it familiar? When do you go to this posture?

- Note how this was created. What triggers you to want to go to this posture? Are there inner meanings/voices that you know from the past such as "stand up straight"?

- Let yourself become still with this exploration and notice if there is a desire to make a change in this posture. See if you can resist making a big change, but rather allow very small and incremental movements to make this change. How would you need to move right now to lengthen your spine? How does your body want to make a change? See if you can follow the small shifts.

- Allow your spine to lengthen, not straighten! Imagine that the top of your head is gently lifted like the end of a string of pearls. Imagine that the bottom of your spine is gently dropping towards the ground like an anchor. Soften your knees. Allow your breath to be soft and steady.

- Feel the spine lengthen on its own. Track the feelings that go with it. *(Note: If the client has trouble making this shift, you can enhance the imagery such as "lift through the crown of the head," etc. Or you can gently place your hand on the top of their head and have them push gently upward so they can feel a lengthening sensation through the gentle resistance.)*

- Now that you are standing long and tall, notice how the rest of the body wants to follow this alignment. Find the natural expression of your body posture right now. Take a moment to feel this new posture. What feelings and sensations go with this?

- Has your mood shifted? What are you in touch with now? Discuss what has changed and how you can repeat this process from the inside-out when you notice the collapsed posture.

- With a lengthy spine I sense and feel in my body:_____

_____

client exercise

Grounding Through the Spine

PURPOSE

Working with the awareness of the spine is an easy way to ground the client. Clients working with stress or trauma activation can experience spacing out, not feeling present, physical tiredness, or a collapsed body posture. This exercise guides the client through a mindful awareness of the spine aligning and straightening, bringing back a sense of inner alignment and presence. This can be done sitting or standing. By straightening the spine mindfully, the client is able to shift their inner state and open up to a more balanced experience. In the more aligned posture, it will be easier to talk out how collapsed they were previously. This also teaches a direct somatic path towards bringing oneself out of a low-mood state.

Note to therapist:

When you notice that the client feels collapsed in the body, as if sunken into themselves (such as a collapsed chest, a rounded spine, and the head hanging forward with a flat affect), you might try this intervention.

INSTRUCTIONS

- Invite the client to notice their current body posture: "Notice how you are sitting right now. What are you aware of?"
- Invite the client to experiment with changing this posture by slowly shifting the spine: "Let yourself very slowly and mindfully straighten your spine by stacking one vertebra on top of the next. Take your time and notice how you can move the spine into an upright position, from the bottom to the neck."
- Make sure you talk the client through this slowly, as you want them to be aware of the shift that is occurring: "Go ahead and slowly stack the spine and notice the change that is happening as you do this."
- You might have to invite them to repeat this movement, as most people do it too quickly and think of the end result rather than the process of stacking the spine.
- Encourage the natural curve of the spine and not a "stiff" spine. This is about straightening and aligning the spine. Use instructional words such as: lengthening, lifting, reaching up, moving your spine towards the space above the head.
- You can use imagery such as: "Imagine you are being gently pulled by a string from the top of your head, your spine being a string of pearls that is being gently lifted." Or, "Imagine your spine growing upwards."
- If touch is permitted, you can gently place a flat hand on the top of the head and apply a gentle pressure, to which the client can push upwards towards the hand and pressure. This gives a more direct feedback and makes it easy to align the spine. Once the spine is straight, remove the hand.
- Once the client has straightened their spine, have them pause and notice what the change is like: "What do you notice now? What is it like to sense your world from this vantage point? How does it feel right now?"
- Track for eye contact, a relaxation of breath, and a brightness of mood.
- Have the client dwell in this posture so they can internally mark the change. Here the client can notice how "sunken," or "collapsed" they were previously.

client exercise

Inner Alignment

"Kinesthesia, the feeling of movement and of weight, is the important source of our information."
—Mabel Todd, *The Thinking Body*

PURPOSE

This exercise is to establish a kinesthetic sense and feel of inner alignment. Sensing one's inner alignment creates a sense of groundedness in the body.

INSTRUCTIONS

- Sit upright on a chair or cushion, either cross-legged or with your legs on the ground. If you are cross-legged, then make sure your pelvis is not tucked.

- Take a moment to sense into your spine by rocking gently back and forth to feel where the "middle" of your posture is.

- Notice any temptation to want to straighten your spine, or push it forward or back from a sense of "outer" viewing of your body.

- Slow down so you can sense and feel your body. Close your eyes.

- Imagine a column or beam of light that moves from the top of your head all the way to your seat. This column is right in the center of your body.

- Take a moment to sense and visualize this column, and then notice how the body wants to organize around this center column. Notice small shifts in the body, adjusting. Let that happen.

- Let the breath be natural and easy. You are letting the body be relaxed, and at the same time notice how, by visualizing this column, you are making small inner shifts in your posture.

- Let this happen until you feel an inner alignment; this can be a sense of calm, being centered, slowed down, or an awareness of your whole body being relaxed and alert at the same time.

- Linger here for a few more moments and then ask: What does my body feel like right now?

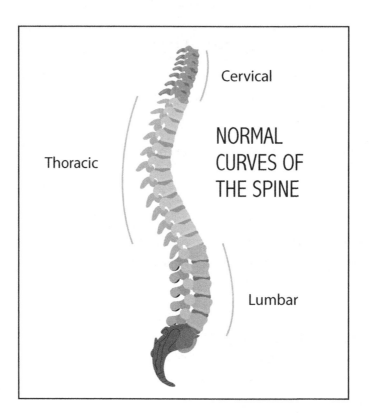

Make sure your sitting posture is aligned. You want the spine to have a natural curve and be upright. Avoid slouching and collapsing the posture.

Somatic Strength Posture

client exercise

PURPOSE

Research on the effects of assuming a power posture for a short time show a resulting increase in hormone levels. Assuming a strength-based posture for a short two minutes, with shoulders up, the spine erect, and the chin high, will produce elevated testosterone in the body. This extra boost from your own biology will raise your emotional confidence. In somatic work, assuming a more confident posture and "embodying it" makes a big emotional difference. You will feel more engaged and lifted, and positive emotions have a chance to balance out the self-doubt and self-criticism. Assuming strength in your physical posture is the highlight in this tool.

A posture change boosts the mood and changes the "scene." This is a good, quick technique when the client is working on confidence issues, performance anxiety, or mood changes. Working on posture change also is a way to feel your own boundaries. When you are more confident and in your strength, you are more likely to have appropriate/healthy boundaries. You can practice this posture in a playful way with the client to help them learn how to do this for themselves at home. Teach your client that they can assume this posture for two minutes when they recognize they are down or need a boost in confidence.

This is different from noticing the kind of posture the client inhabits most of the time. The key here is not just to assume a strength posture, but to become aware when they are not confident and how the physical posture mirrors the internal experience.

INSTRUCTIONS

- Stand and notice your posture right now, as it is. Don't make a change yet.

- Now shift your awareness into standing tall and straight (with a natural curve in the spine), placing your feet firmly on the ground. Lift your arms overhead and stretch them out. Imagine you are reaching for something above.

- Lift your head slightly upwards.

- Sense into this posture you are taking right now. Feel the strength of this posture. If you don't, make slight adjustments until you do.

- Hold the posture for a short while. You want to hold this posture until you feel your arms getting tired or you need to shift. No longer than two to three minutes.

- Bring your arms down, relax and assume a normal body posture.

- Notice any change. Maybe your mood is slightly different? What subtle changes can you sense right now?

- You might repeat this a couple more times. Track for the small changes in affect. A lighter mood, a silliness, or a smile indicate that the posture exercise has worked.

- Experiment with what your confidence posture is.

Reflection:

My confidence posture is:

_____

My areas to work on in my posture are:

_____

_____

_____

therapist
worksheet

Posture Snapshot

PURPOSE

This is a body-reading tool to help you learn how to see and perceive your client's body from a somatic perspective. You can do this when the client first walks into the office, or when you sense that you need a fresh perspective on the client.

Important note:
Body readings are educated guesses and not truths. They need to be checked out with the client's experience. Be willing to be wrong.

INSTRUCTIONS

- Close your eyes very briefly, as if you were a camera.
- Take three quick snapshots, letting your eyes fall on different areas of the body.
- Write down the first impression, without any judgment, of what you see.

First Snapshot:	Second Snapshot:
1. I see	1. I see
_____	_____
2. I imagine	2. I imagine
_____	_____
3. I am curious about	3. I am curious about
_____	_____

Third Snapshot:	What my body reading is:
1. I see	_____
_____	
2. I imagine	_____
_____	
3. I am curious about	_____
_____	

Draw Your Skeleton

PURPOSE

Our skeleton is part of our posture. We never see or feel into our skeleton. To correct our posture and feel alignment from the inside, let's imagine your skeleton. This does not have to be anatomically correct.

INSTRUCTIONS

Draw a picture of the front, side, and back of your skeleton using the three boxes below.

My Skeleton:

FRONT   SIDE   BACK

Reflection:

Reflect on how the skeleton you drew holds you up.

What kind of inner alignment do you imagine is based on this skeleton?

Find a word or phrase to describe it: _____

CHAPTER 16
Gesture and Non-Verbal Communication

NON-VERBAL COMMUNICATION

Only 30-40% of our human interactions are communicated verbally. The majority of our communications are non-verbal. The body becomes the running commentator of how and what we feel in our exchanges. Paying attention to gestures such as body posture, language use, and movement, become essential cues to help therapists understand the client's experience in context. No single body cue can be understood alone. The challenge is to read the body expression accurately and without bias, so we can use this information in the therapeutic work towards awareness and growth.

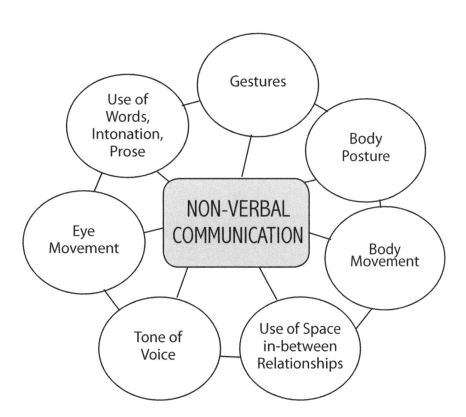

therapist worksheet

Non-Verbal Communications Chart

INSTRUCTIONS

Chart your observation of the client's non-verbal communications. This worksheet highlights what you observe and helps you track what needs improvement.

Posture
- ☐ Upright
- ☐ Stiff
- ☐ Slouching

Gesture
- ☐ Expressive
- ☐ Non-Expressive

Body Movement
- ☐ Rocking
- ☐ Fidgeting
- ☐ Still

Talking
- ☐ Pausing
- ☐ Rapid
- ☐ Slow

Eye Movement
- ☐ Scanning
- ☐ Focused
- ☐ Withdrawn
- ☐ Intrusive

Tone Of Voice
- ☐ High Pitch
- ☐ Low Pitch
- ☐ Pressed

CATEGORIES OF NON-VERBAL COMMUNICATION

Spatial Use
- ☐ Appropriate
- ☐ Too Close
- ☐ Too Far Apart

Sounds
- ☐ Nervous
- ☐ Laughter
- ☐ Umm, Ahh's

Head Movement
- ☐ Yes Nodding
- ☐ No Side to Side

Appearance
- ☐ Tidy
- ☐ Untidy

Body Contact
- ☐ Seeks Contact
- ☐ Avoids Contact
- ☐ Slow

Use Of Words
- ☐ Dramatic
- ☐ Pauses
- ☐ Monotone

Facial Expression
- ☐ Tight & Held
- ☐ Frown
- ☐ Open/Relaxed

therapist worksheet

Tracking the Meaning of Gestures

PURPOSE

Gestures are part of the non-verbal communications system. A gesture communicates in tandem with facial and body expressions to reveal a person's feelings or inner mood. Gestures are unconscious communicators of the body. If read correctly, they can convey to the therapist what is truthful in the client's experience. When reading these gestures, you can comment on them in order to help the client become more aware of themselves. It is important to be non-judging and gentle when making observations.

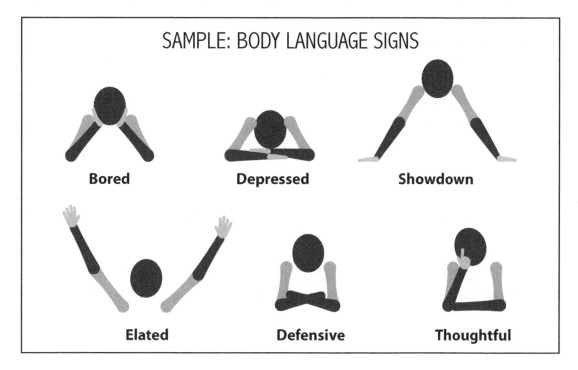

SAMPLE: BODY LANGUAGE SIGNS

Bored   Depressed   Showdown

Elated   Defensive   Thoughtful

INSTRUCTIONS

This chart on page 160 is a systematic way of observing a gesture and putting it together with what you hear and sense so you can involve the client in exploring other options in their somatic sense.

Steps:

- Write down:
    1) What you observe.
    2) What the client reported.
    3) What the client's mood or emotion was at that time.
- Reflect on these three aspects and form a "hunch."

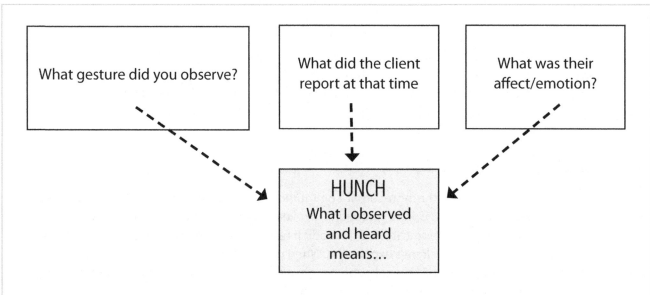

After your hunch is formed, confirm your hunch with a follow-up comment such as: "I noticed that your shoulders moved up as you talked about your friend. You also seemed a little fearful. What is happening right now in your body?"

GESTURE	REPORT

EMOTION	HUNCH

- Finish by asking the client the following questions:
  1) What needs to happen right now?
  2) Now that you are aware of this, what shift can you make in your body right now?

Centered Hands

PURPOSE

Centering hands is a quick way to bring the attention into the body. This focus brings awareness to the body in a non-threatening way. It's an easy exercise for the client to practice at home.

INSTRUCTIONS

This can be done sitting or standing. The instructions below are for a standing position, but you can modify them accordingly.

- Stand tall and aligned. Have your feet wider than your hips for stability.

- Close your eyes (if you are comfortable) so you can switch more to feeling your body from the inside.

- Stretch your arms wide, as if you are stretching out eagle wings. Keep your arms level with your shoulders as you stretch.

- Keep your head in alignment and resist the urge to tilt your head back.

- When you can't stretch out sideways any longer, VERY SLOWLY bring your arms towards the center of your chest.

- Curl your fingers; have the fingertips lead the way back towards the center of your chest. Let the hands follow on the level of the chest, and bring the hands towards each other.

- You have a few options here: You can have your hands touching each other, or fold them in a prayer position, or rest them on the chest. Notice how each position has a different effect. You can experiment with what feels right to you.

- Dwell on this meeting point of your hands and chest.

- Take five slow, deep breaths. Notice how your hands and chest move as you breathe.

- Notice how the touching of the hands begins to center your body.

- Pay attention to your lower belly, your feet and your overall body.

- Then drop your arms by your sides and notice.

- Repeat this movement no more than three times. You can alter the hand position, varying between touching hands or resting them on the chest, and notice the effect.

Reflection:

- What is your internal experience right now?

- What needs meeting or grounding in your life?

Notes: _____

_____

_____

client
exercise

Midline Gestures

PURPOSE

This exercise guides the client to the midline of the body in order to balance and ground them. Developing infants, for instance, learn to cross their hand movements over their midline in order to become more organized in their movement patterns.

The midline can be thought of as an energy line that runs vertically through the center of the body. In fact, both martial arts and Chinese medicine perceive this midline as the energetic center of the body. It touches the solar plexus, the navel and the lower Dantian—the area from which our sense of groundedness and well-being radiate. The lower Dantian is found by placing two fingers below the navel, along the midline. The lower Dantian is the energy center of the body.

If a client's movement is disorganized (meaning their arm and hand movements are not coordinated with the rest of the body), this exercise might also be beneficial to increase the body awareness of their midline. Think of the midline awareness as a deep organizer of one's body feeling.

INSTRUCTIONS

- Stand up. Align your posture: Hips underneath the shoulders, head aligned with the shoulder girdle.
- Ground your feet through the earth.
- Touch your crown briefly.
- Touch your solar plexus briefly.
- Touch your navel.
- Touch your Dantian.
- Then hold your hands on the Dantian. Breathe slowly into this point.
- Imagine a line from the crown to the Dantian.
- Gently pivot around this midline. Use very small movements, so you get a sense of the midline.
- Come to a stillness and feel into the midline.

Reflection:
- Ask your client to reflect on the effect on this exercise.
    1. What is your physical stance right now?
    2. What do you notice in your body?
    3. How do you experience the midline?
    4. What effect is this exercise having right now?

CHAPTER 17
Emotions and Self-Regulation

SOMA, EMOTIONS AND THE ART OF SELF-REGULATION

Part of a healthy body-mind connection is understanding our body's signals and needs. When we develop as young children, our needs are met and regulated by adults. We learn to internalize how to care for ourselves by the way we have been cared for.

The caring touch, the empathic embrace, or the comforting voice of a kind parent helps us learn to self-regulate when we have strong emotions or are stressed. When the body learns that stressed moments or dysregulated body states such as thirst and hunger are not met, or are met with aggression, fear or threat, these regulating functions do not get appropriately internalized. The result is irritability and misunderstood or confusing body symptoms, that can result in anxiety or depression.

Learning to recognize the need for self-regulation and re-learning the responses towards distress and stress are critical in health and well-being. Healthy self-regulation is knowing one's body, learning to read one's body signals, and knowing what to do when the stressors get high. The more we learn how to enhance our self-regulating capacity, the more resourcefully and creatively we can deal with life challenges.

When we can improve our self-regulation, we also improve learning how to cope and be with a range of emotions. Functioning self-regulation is dependent on a strong thinking capacity, the ability to be aware and be reflective of one's actions, thoughts and behaviors. This top-down strength of the prefrontal cortex can be enhanced by cultivating a strong somatic sense of self. The more the client can embody their experience and regulate their physical body, the stronger the mental capacity. As described in the following tools, learning how to be in tune with the body can enhance self-regulating capacities. The happier the body is, the more spacious the mind and the more thoughtful the emotional decisions and behaviors we undertake.

client
worksheet

Meaning Making: High-Road vs. Low-Road

How do you create meaning based on your experiences? Do you rely primarily on the reasoning mind (the high-road), or do you depend mostly on the information you receive from your body-based emotional experiences? The low-road is referred to when we instinctively respond to a situation. This is often in a traumatic or stressful situation when we engage the fight or flight response. But the low-road can also be an instinctive response that is well tuned to a situation or experience.

Do you use a combination of both the high and low roads to bring meaning and process your experiences and life?

Often these meaning-making modes are not recognized, but rather instinctual or based on a "feeling," a "sense," or a "gut feeling." Becoming aware of how we create meanings is crucial to understanding our direct somatic experience.

We want to notice when a fear overrides the reasoning brain and learn the mindful and somatic techniques to integrate, regulate, and calm. We want to understand that the prefrontal cortex can help us out when we are emotional, and use thinking strategies to get through confusion or decision-making. Understanding where our basic physiology intersects with our body is part of understanding our whole human experience. Decisions are based on the meaning you attach to them. Reflect on the various ways you can make decisions and attach meaning to those decisions. What do you value most? How does your body or your mind respond? Do they respond in tandem? What is that process for you?

Reflection:

Think of a time when you made a calm and reasonable decision. How did you do this? What did that feel like?_____

_____

Think of a time when you made an "emotional decision." What did that feel like? In hindsight it was a good decision or a poor one?_____

_____

Think of a time when you made a body-based and instinctual decision. What did that feel like? How do you evaluate that decision in hindsight?_____

_____

What do you consider as a good decision and what meaning do you attach to it?

_____

client
worksheet

Emotions Chart - Self-Assessment and Emotional Themes

INSTRUCTIONS

Use the chart below to assess your emotional life and core thoughts and beliefs. Reflect on the main themes that govern your life. On a scale from one to 10, rate where you are at with each core theme. Take a moment to sense and feel them in your body before writing down the number. Then circle the correlating belief that most fits your experience.

1 - LESS ⬅ ━ ━ ━ ━ ━ ━ ━ ━ ━ ━ ➡ 10 - MORE

Positive Beliefs	Theme	Negative Beliefs	My Rating
I am connected I feel safe I belong I am in my body	**Theme of Safety and Belonging**	I feel isolated I don't belong I am not safe	
I am supported Others care about me I can rely on others My needs matter	**Theme of Dependency**	No one cares I can't rely on others My needs don't matter I don't have needs	
I am free to be and act I am a good person I am creative and spontaneous	**Theme of Independence**	I am trapped My impulses hurt others I can't get my way I am a bad person	
I am truthful and authentic It's safe to be real It's okay to be vulnerable with others	**Theme of Truth**	I can't be weak If I am real, I will be shamed I am used, not loved	
I am loved for who I am I am centered and peaceful I am worthy of love and attention I add value	**Theme of Worth**	I am not good enough Love has to be earned Something is wrong with me I have to prove my worthiness	

Reflection:

Identify the core themes on this chart. Reflect on how these themes impact your life and your somatic life. How has this shaped your experience in your body?

Notes: _____

_____

client
exercise

Lean Back to Lean In

PURPOSE

This exercise is a short practice to work with irritation, impatience or emotional agitation in the moment. It is designed to help the client work with their impulse-control issues. If a client has a tendency to quickly jump into a conversation or an action, have them practice this tool. The outcome is a calmer and more rational manner of engaging without being reactive.

Practice this with your client in the office first to help establish a good habit. After a few practices, the client will be able to do this for themselves. Convey the importance of repetition. This is a powerful yet simple self-regulation tool the client can add to their daily living.

INSTRUCTIONS

This is a short two-minute exercise.

- Notice the feeling of irritation, impatience, or tension in the body.

- Check into your body posture: Are you leaning forward? Are the muscles in your belly clenched? Is your face straining or tense? Are your eyes straining or tense? Is your voice hurried or high pitched? Is your head down as if you are fighting a strong wind?

- Time to lean back!

- Stop what you are doing and shift your body posture into a leaning-back posture. This can be sitting back or shifting your weight backwards while standing. If you are standing, sense your heels rather than the balls of your feet. If you are sitting, feel the back of the chair; sense your sitting bones.

- Let you gaze be relaxed. Imagine you are looking from behind your eyes, as if you are dropping backwards into your eyes. This will allow you to take in the whole vista in front of you without straining forward. You might gently look around and move your eyes and head slowly as if you are scanning the horizon.

- Do this for one to two minutes.

- Notice what changes. Was there a small mood shift? Did you notice a detail you hadn't before? How is your mood now? Do you still want to react? Or can you pass on that urge?

Now that you've learned how to lean back, you can choose what to lean in to!

Reflection:

What was my reactivity to wanting to act quickly?

What triggered the impulsivity?

What do I really want to lean in to?

What is important?

Managing the "Too Much"

PURPOSE

This exercise will help the client manage a situation, an arousal in the body, a floating feeling or any experience that feels "too much." By bite-sizing the experience, you are teaching the client how to manage a situation they have perceived as un-manageable. This new ability to manage an experience then creates a new perspective that they are capable of dealing with emotions as well. This exercise is a good focusing tool. It brings the client into the present moment and helps them become more aware of what is important.

INSTRUCTIONS

Sitting down comfortably:

- Close your eyes.

- Connect with your body and breath.

- Then open and close your eyes quickly, as if you are taking a snapshot with your eyes.

- Harvest the moment right after. Notice what your experience is.

- What detail is in the foreground? What stands out?

- Take another snapshot.

- What did your eyes land on this time? The same place? Different details? What is curious to you now?

- Take a third snapshot.

- What is your body feeling? Are you more aware of your body right now? What is alive in you?

- Open your eyes. Notice what changes are present. Do you feel overwhelmed? Do you feel you can handle your situation?

Walking in the room, slowly:

- Start standing. Tune into your body; take a baseline of where you are at.

- Take a few slow steps. Make sure you have an unobstructed path in front of you.

- Take a snapshot while you are walking. Notice what is curious as you close your eyes. What stays with you?

- Take another snapshot. This time, notice what detail you are seeing in your mind's eye.

- Turn your head and take another snapshot. See what surprises you. Linger with the imprint as you slowly continue walking.

- Repeat this one to two times more. Walk slowly and turn your head so each time you have a fresh surprise on what your eyes are capturing.

- Take time to linger with your eyes closed after you've finishing taking the snapshots.

- Stand still and process and digest the experience.

- Notice how much easier it is to be with one thing at a time. Notice your body's response.

Reflection:

Imagine taking snapshots of your emotional life. You can learn to regulate your overwhelm or stress by using the snapshot technique when you are feeling something too strongly. Can you bite-size your experience enough so it becomes manageable? How can you do this?

Sailing the Midline

PURPOSE

Visualize a sailboat crisscrossing a midline. Every time it goes off course, it corrects and comes back towards the midline. This midline is a metaphor for our grounded being-ness. This exercise teaches you how to come back when you feel "off course" by using the midline of your body. The midline represents the middle of your body, or your core.

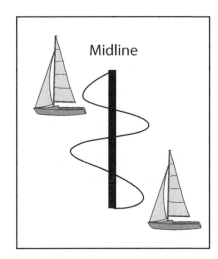

Midline

INSTRUCTIONS

- Stand tall. Have your eyes open and downcast.

- Imagine a midline in the center of your body, from the top of your head down to your feet.

- Notice how you feel "off course." Name it out loud.

I feel off course because: _____

- Now lift your right arm. Turn your palm so it's facing towards the left and stretch it across the imaginary midline of your body so you are crossing your hand and arm in front of your chest.

- Drop your arm and return it to the natural position.

- Now lift your left arm. Turn your palm so it's facing towards the right and cross your hand and arm over the midline until you can't go further. Then drop your arm so it returns to the natural position.

- With each crossing: exhale.

- With each returning to the natural position: inhale.

- Repeat this movement slowly and deliberately six to eight times.

- Stand and notice what is happening in your body. Are you calm? Grounded? More aware? Focused?

My body now feels: _____

client
exercise

Sitting Run

PURPOSE

You can use a simple sitting-run exercise to down-regulate anxious and nervous energy in the body. This exercise engages the two hemispheres of the brain and creates a bilateral stimulation of both hemispheres. This causes a unifying experience in the body, rather than a discomforting one. During this exercise you will stay seated, which makes it more comfortable and manageable. Simply "walk in the chair" and watch your breath slow down.

You can use this seated walking motion anytime in your life you sense anxious feelings arise. This is a good body training that turns your attention away from familiar triggers and discharges tension.

INSTRUCTIONS

- Start by sitting in a chair.

- Begin "walking your legs" by gently pushing into your shoes and into the ground, one leg and one foot at a time. A small pivoting motion will start happening in your hips, as if you are walking. Let that motion happen as naturally as you can.

- Take one foot, push it into the ground; then the other. Repeat this motion and synchronize your breath. Ideally you want to exhale while you push into the ground. Make sure you don't stiffen your legs, but keep an easy walking pace.

- Pay attention to what happens. Is your breath slowing down? Is the anxiety or nervous energy calming down?

CHAPTER 18
Body and Self-Image

Body and self-image are often what we come up against when working somatically. Culturally, we are trained to view ourselves from the outside-in rather than valuing what we feel inside. We learn to see ourselves through the eyes of others; this internalizes negative messages and self-beliefs. Examining the body image and how we are naming ourselves is an important lesson in learning how to work with the body.

Body Image - Inside-Out vs. Outside-In

PURPOSE

This exercise transforms the awareness of our over-reliance on how one "looks" and is perceived by others. The discomfort of self-image creates self-consciousness and comparison with others. This reflection exercise asks the client to kindly observe the outer perceptions of their body and shift the reference to the inner felt sense of the body that is not determined by others.

The reflection questions provided are meant to inspire an honest look at the use of our inner critic on the body. How can you shift from the outer perception of your body to a stable inner perception? Be patient. This will take time as you need to not only change how you think, but also how you think in tandem with how you feel and sense yourself. The change comes when we "FEEL" different in our bodies and that inner truth becomes stronger than how we "PERCEIVE" our bodies.

INSTRUCTIONS

Reflection questions on the outer perception:

- What do you call your body?

  _____

- Do you have names for your body parts?

  _____

- How often do you view yourself in the mirror or in pictures and critique yourself?

  _____

- How do you feel after such self-viewing?

  _____

- Do you check your social media for positive reflections on your looks?

  _____

- When you get a review on your looks, what happens? Do you feel satisfied, happy? Does this inspire you towards change? What kind?

  _____

- If you had a magic wish, what would you change in your body?

  _____

- What would the change bring you?

  _____

client exercise

Shifting the Perception

PURPOSE

This exercise is the second part of the Tool 84: Body Image – Inside-Out vs. Outside-In exercise. This part can be done at home alone or in the office with the help of the therapist, whichever is more comfortable. It can also be modified according to your comfort level.

INSTRUCTIONS

If you are guiding your client, ask them to so slow down their breath. Direct them to sense and feel their body. Adopt a caring tone of voice.

- Identify the posture in which you feel most self-conscious: sitting, standing, laying down.

- Take this position and place yourself in front of a mirror.

- Start with your eyes closed. Don't look into the mirror at first.

- In your self-conscious posture, <u>"FEEL" into your body first.</u>

- As you feel your body, tune into the rhythm of your breath, and the sensations of your posture; find the comfort of your posture. Settle in and stay for a few moments. Make this posture safe! Use a safe image if you like, such as a nature image, a loving person, animal, etc.

- Take a very quick peek at the mirror, like a photo lens opening up, and close your eyes again.

- Be with the aftermath of this image; study it. Commit yourself to sensing and feeling the body as you take in the image you glanced at.

- Notice the negative voices coming up, the self-conscious messages; the shuttle to the ACTUAL SENSATIONS and FEEL of the body.

- Is the outer perception true right now?

- Continue this process for three to four more glances. Each time you are waiving the self-conscious imprint in favor of the actual experience you are having in the body.

- Notice any small changes in your perception. Be patient and celebrate any small change you see and feel. Over time this exercise will bring you the benefit of a perception change.

- Repeat this exercise several times a week. Use the timetable on the next page to note any changes.

Perception Log

Time	Monday	Tuesday	Wednesday	Thursday	Friday	Saturday	Sunday
AM							
PM							
Worked with body parts							
Perception change							

Body Drawing

PURPOSE

Body drawing is a way to express and assess where you are internally. The key is to not overthink the drawing, but to allow the body wisdom to come through directly.

INSTRUCTIONS

- You can use colored markers or pens for this exercise.

- Where are you right now? Make a quick drawing. Don't think; just draw what comes to mind first.

Look at your drawing and title it. Use the first phrase that comes into your mind. Write it below.

_____

- Now, look at an aspect of your drawing and then pick out a color, shape or something interesting and draw that piece again. Think of it as magnifying an aspect of your first drawing.

- Take a look at the new drawing. Title it, using the first phrase or words that come up.

_____

- With the two drawings and titles, take a moment and reflect quietly on what this means to you right now. What are you discovering?

_____

_____

_____

You can journal your response or express it in a final drawing.

client
exercise

Breathing into the Seven Energy Centers

PURPOSE

An ancient system of seven energy centers in the body—originally developed in India—provides a lens through which we can restore well-being. We can touch these seven energy centers, or chakras, by imagination, breath and sensation. Your body-image health arises from engaging with the seven centers in a gentle way so you can feel the alignment of your inner body. By simply placing your awareness and using self-touch, you can work with your own energy. Use the chart to help you visualize each energy center as you move through the instructions. For the purposes of this book the energy centers serve as an awareness to anchor the client's mind to the body. This tool is to highlight the inner perception of one's body.

Note to therapist:

This is a guided visualization by the therapist, the script is on page 182. You can record this for the client to listen to later. It works well if the client can repeat this exercise with your voice later on. You also want to make sure that the idea of chakras is congruent with the client's religious background and beliefs. One way to translate the word "chakra" for clients who do not align with this language is to offer breathing into the places in the body along the center line of their body axis.

As the client gets comfortable with imagining the colors, you can encourage them to imagine their own colors. The focus in on strengthening the inner perception of the body.

Energy Centers Chart:

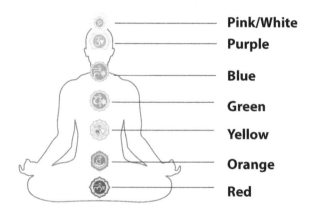

Pink/White
Purple
Blue
Green
Yellow
Orange
Red

1. Red - The Base Energy: Getting connected with being grounded

2. Orange - The Lower Belly Energy: Open to new experiences and inner abundance

3. Yellow - Upper Center Energy: Ability to be confident and in control of your life, free from the judgments of others

4. Green - Heart Center: Connect with love and inner joy, compassion

5. Blue - Throat Center: Communicate truth and mindfulness

6. Purple - Forehead Center: Focus and see the big picture

7. Pink/White - Crown Energy: Open to your inner purpose, calm and wisdom

INSTRUCTIONS

Set up:

Identify an area that is interesting or troubling for the client. For example, the client might experience a tightness in their lower abdomen. You can start with the exercise in that area alone and then include the other energy centers later. Although this exercise is laid out sequentially, it can be done out of order if you are working on one specific energy center. Modify it to your client's needs.

You can also give this as a homework assignment. Encourage the client to work with the challenged area and focus on it.

- Sequence from the bottom to the top energy centers in order.

- Begin by having the client visualize the color and the region of the body.

- Ask them to place their hand on that part of the body.

- Gently guide them to breathe into that region and hold the image of the color.

- Instruct your client to go through the sequence of the colors as you call them out, each time sliding their hand to the area they are working in.

- Hold each area for two to three breaths before moving on. You want a fluid cycling through the centers.

- Debrief the experience. Focus on what was easy and what was challenging. What can be changed? What can be added?

- If you have identified an area of challenge, you can repeat the instructions, focusing on that area specifically. Notice the changes.

Script:

In a calm and steady voice, guide the client through the sequence:

1. Move your attention to the red center of your body. Take a breath here. Visualize the color at the base of your seat. Allow your attention to sink in. See if you can find a connection here with this part of your body. Don't force anything, just simply dwell with the color and the breath in your seat. Reflect on the theme of how grounded you are. How can you shift into your most grounded sense of self right now? What needs to happen here for you to feel the connection with the earth?

2. Now move your inner attention to the orange center: the lower belly. Bring your breath here. Take slow inhales and exhales and hold the image of the color in your lower belly. Let whatever wants to arise be there. This is an easy access to your breath rhythm. You can reflect on the theme of how deeply abundant you are, what you have and are blessed with. How can you shift into the riches of who you are here?

3. Move your attention now to the yellow center: the solar plexus region. Imagine the color yellow and place your attention on the upper belly region. Take slow breaths in this area and feel the expansion of the breath as it touches the side ribs and upper belly region. Let your focus rest here. You can reflect here on the theme of freeing yourself from other people's opinions and judgments of you. What does it take to return to your own inner judgment, free from others?

4. Now move your attention to the green heart center in the center of your chest. Breathe into that center strongly with expansive and slow breaths. Hold the color green here. Place your hand on the heart center and listen quietly. You can reflect on the theme of your loving and compassionate heart. How can you open further to the joy and love in your heart center right now?

5. Move your attention now to the blue energy center in your throat. Bring the color blue to mind as you sense into your throat area. Bring your breath awareness to this region. Reflect on how you express yourself. Do you use your words mindfully? Do you communicate with truth and care?

6. Move your attention on to the purple energy center in your forehead. Place your focus and breath awareness between your eyebrows. Let your attention settle here. Take a moment. Bring to mind the totality of your life. Make a grand sweep over all aspects of your life: work, relationships, spirituality, and your challenges and joys. Take a big step back and don't get drawn into any details. Keep the focus on the forehead center and see what rises here right now.

7. Now move your attention to the pink/white energy center. Bring your awareness to the crown of your head. Breathe into the skull. See if you can sense small subtle movements here. Bring calm and stability here. Take steady and calm inhales and exhales. Stay with the experience that is and don't reflect actively on anything. Just stay open for a few moments and see what comes up.

CHAPTER 19
Breath Awareness and Techniques

GUIDELINES WHEN WORKING WITH BREATH

Working with breath is a powerful somatic tool. There are two aspects: 1) diagnosing where the client is at by tracking the breath, and 2) teaching the client breathing techniques for intervention.

As a somatic therapist, you always want to track the breath quality of the client. Learn how to listen to, and see, the breath in the body. Open your awareness to include the breath quality of your client and reflect on how they are breathing when they are talking, exploring a theme, or experiencing emotions. This will give you insight and ideas on how to help your clients. Here are some basic guidelines when working with breath:

1. Track the breath quality, rhythm and location

2. Assess for hyper or hypo condition

3. Assess for need to interrupt, calm, redirect, or increase

- Preview the breath. Explain ahead of time what you are doing and possibly guide the client through the exercise.

- Explain any instructions in simple terms.

- Set up breathing like an experiment. (Just suggesting a breath experiment or even placing an awareness on the breath can elicit a response.)

- Always suggest "kind" breath interventions. Never push or force any breath experiments.

- Have the client rehearse the breath activity first. Have them try it once and give feedback. Then make adjustments based on the feedback.

- Practice breath once and then pause to check and modify.

- Modify to their needs and level of activation.

- Track for any increases or decreases in emotional or traumatic activation levels. Make adjustments if you are tracking traumatic activation.

- Practice the breath along with client.

- Ask them to be in open attention and notice the effect of the breath. You can ask simply, "What do you notice now?"

- If they move out of mindfulness, guide them gently back into mindfulness: "See if you can return inward."

- Always make it smaller and gentler and more manageable (never push!).

- Look for successful moments and make contact with these moments: "You really had a strong breath that went all the way into the lower belly."

- You are re-educating this nervous system, not challenging it.

- Debrief on the effects of the experiment.

- You can do breathing integration when walking, sitting, or moving with impulses.

- Give the client breathing protocols for homework; design it with them. Write it down or record it for them to repeat at home.

THE TRUTH ABOUT DEEP BREATHING

Often the first intervention a non-somatic therapist will suggest when noticing anxiety or panic trying to intervene into a client's body, is to have them "take deep breaths." Deep breathing is a wonderful and regulating activity; done correctly it can be very helpful for the client. But what is often missing are a few key ingredients and set-ups.

1. Therapist—you must stay calm and breathe yourself! Nothing is worse than an agitated voice that gives a stern instruction to breathe deeply.

2. Pick the client up where they are at. ACKNOWLEDGE THEM! For example: "I notice your breathing is shallow." "It's kind of hard to breathe right now, huh?" "Is it difficult to catch your breath?" You will not make it worse, which is the assumption, but you will actually start the regulation right there and then. The client wants to be seen when they're breathing strangely, so they can get help from you at that moment.

3. Bitesize! Suggest small breathing experiments first. For example: "Try breathing into the sides of your body near the ribs and belly…" "Why don't you notice how the inhale is larger than the exhale?" "How about slowing the breath a little bit?" "Where does the breath want to go right now?"

4. Track, track, track. Whenever breath is shallow, fast, panicky, filled with anxiety or very low energy, you want to track the associated emotions and mental state along with it. Breath is never isolated from the rest of the experience. Make contact with the whole experience. For example: "You seem to be feeling a little down." "Seems like a lot of fears are coming up." "You appear uncomfortable right now..."

5. Suggest breathing techniques the client can do. Set them up for success. When they master one breath, they feel inspired and in control. Anxious breath FEELS inside as being out of control. Suggest breathing techniques that bring them back to self-control and mastery.

6. Use a calm and reassuring voice in your instructions. The client's awareness is heightened and your voice is amplified in that moment. Stay calm!

7. Use language such as: "Take a deeper breath." "See where the breath wants to land right now." "How can you extend this inhale/exhale?" "What do you need to do to change this breath right now?"

8. Avoid saying: "Take deep belly breaths." Instead say: "Put your hand on your belly and see if you can bring more volume into the belly. See what you can do with your breath right now."

HOW TO USE THE BREATHING TOOLS

You might wonder which breathing tool is right for your client. Which tool should you start with? As with any somatic intervention tool, you need to use your common sense in conjunction with the data that you are tracking from the client's body cues. If you notice the client is breathing quickly, a tool that brings forth calm and regulation, such as Tool #89: Breathing Towards Calm, will be useful. If you perceive that the client is more anxious, Tool # 93: Deflating the Tire of Anxiety will be beneficial. If the client needs an introduction to breathing awareness, Tool #91: Three-Part Breathing Sequence and Tool #88: Round-Wave Breath are good starting breathing techniques. These tools do not need be used in progression. You want to familiarize yourself with the tools so you can have them at your fingertips when needed.

You can skip around and use the tools as you see fit for your client's needs. As with any somatic tools, you want the feedback from your client to guide you in what works and what doesn't. Learning from your client is key in this process.

client
exercise

Round-Wave Breath

PURPOSE

Breathing like a rounded wave is a quality of breath that initiates the parasympathetic response towards relaxation and rest. This practice teaches the client to actively bring their breath to a quieter space.

Because this exercise induces the parasympathetic breath towards calming, this is a breath you can teach your clients when they need to learn how to calm themselves.

INSTRUCTIONS

- Notice the quality of your breath now.

- Inhale naturally.

- At the top of the inhale, imagine the breath having a rounded quality, almost as if the inhale rolls over into the exhale.

- You can imagine water going over a stone when you have the top breath rounding. Or a gentle wave cresting. You want to focus on the rounding quality of water.

- Focus on the smooth quality of this breath and how it rolls from the inhale into the exhale; let your exhale come to its natural ending.

- Do four to five breaths, then pause and notice any change. You are looking for parasympathetic cues, such as a deeper inhale in the chest or a slowed exhale.

- If necessary, do another round.

Note to therapist:

"Walk" your client through this exercise by tracking the breath: "Notice how the inhale comes to its fullness, and then roll it over. Yes, like that. Then gently let the exhale take its calming journey down…"

Breathing Towards Calm - Regulate Your Breath

PURPOSE

This is a quick intervention breath. If you see the client becoming dissociated or activated, you can instruct them to do this breath. The focus is to shift the state they are in and regulate them up or down.

INSTRUCTIONS

Note to therapist:

Talk the client through this exercise; frequently make contact and guide them. Make sure you are tracking their level of dissociation. If the client can't be with the breath, stop and talk about it. Regulate them by having them think and talk "about" the experience. Track for signs that they're becoming regulated and shifting out of the dissociated state.

Some indicators of this shift are:

- Clear voice

- Ability to know where they are at in their inner experience

- Not terrified or overwhelmed

- Able to follow your instructions

- Calming down

- Curiosity and engagement

When you notice this shift, ask them to pause and notice their body and how they have moved from a dissociated to a regulated state.

Steps:

- With eyes open, take a full inhale all the way towards the pubic bone.

- Notice how the breath fills you up.

- When you exhale, make the sound: "Ahhhhhh," or "Phaaaaa."

- Notice how the chest empties and a slight pressure arises in the belly.

- Empty the breath completely but comfortably.

- Take another strong, full inhale and follow it with the sound again as you exhale.

- Repeat until you feel a shift in activation.

- Then say out loud:

    – *"I am breathing in and I calm my body."*

    – *"I am breathing out; I smile."*

    – *"I am breathing in; I calm my mind."*

    – *"I am breathing out; I am back in control."*

- If you feel lightheaded, make the inhale smaller and less full.

- Notice how you are changing right now. Pay attention as you are calming and gaining back control.

- Once the shift happens, take a moment and notice the change.

client
exercise

Lateral Breathing Sequence

PURPOSE

Lateral (sideways) breathing diversifies the breathing repertoire. Most people think of breathing as an up and down activity of the lungs. When there is tension in the body, there can be a tendency to hold the breath and freeze the middle section of the body. By facilitating the breath laterally, you can help facilitate a sense of the three-dimensionality of breathing. Lateral breathing is about fully expanding the breath into the side ribs and full dimensions of the rib cage.

This exercise explores the calming effects of lateral breathing. It is especially beneficial for clients who have difficulty breathing deeply, as they have an easier time doing the lateral breathing. It can be helpful to use the image of the gentle movement of the gills of a fish breathing. This will focus the breathing on the sides of the body and lungs rather than front.

INSTRUCTIONS

- This exercise can be done sitting up or lying down.
- Have the client touch the sides of their body where the ribs are.
- Instruct them to bring in a full breath towards the sides of the body so it begins to stretch into the rib cage. They can imagine the gills of a fish breathing under water, or a bird's wings expanding sideways. The focus is on expanding the breath laterally, rather than front or back.
- If the client can't visualize the images, then ask them to place their hands on the sides of their ribs and gently press with the rhythm of the breath: Squeeze gently while exhaling and relax the squeeze when inhaling.
- As they breathe, have them follow the up and down motion of the ribs opening and closing.
- Keep working with the breath expanding and notice if the client is down-regulating. If so, continue; if not, stop and assess.
- Follow this process for a few minutes and see where it goes.

client exercise

Three-Part Breathing Sequence

PURPOSE

The three-part breathing sequence helps facilitate a smooth breath that regulates emotional or physiological activation, and also brings an awareness of the breath to different parts of the body. This exercise promotes a sense of inner boundary and body control, and also releases emotional tension that is stored in the body. When done slowly and mindfully, the client can be with the arising sensations and feelings in a calm manner. This breathing rhythm lays the groundwork for entering the body somatically, getting comfortable with breathing, and regulating any anxious feelings.

INSTRUCTIONS

This exercise can be done either sitting up or laying down. Make sure to assess when it is too activating for the client. It is important that they breathe slowly and smoothly to facilitate a sense of calm inside and inner boundary.

- Have the client imagine a resource, something that is healing and healthy to them, such as a safe place, the ground or earth.

- With their hands on their lower belly, have them breathe into their lower belly, mid-chest, and upper chest.

- Track for the flow of breath. Ideally it is smooth and easy. If the client gets stuck by holding the breath or tensing, facilitate the flow by naming the place in the body. Encourage them to place their hand on the place they are working on and breathe with more awareness.

- Ask them to do a breath and notice. You can gently remind the client to trust the body. This can be a challenging moment—the tension might feel unnatural. In that moment, your gentle guidance to stay and feel the body and keep breathing is essential.

- Ask the client to pause and notice the sensations that are present. Have them sense into the safety of the place they were imagining. If appropriate, keep going.

- You want to guide the client to breathe through the three regions in an easy manner. The more practice, the easier this tool will be to utilize.

- Make sure that the client cycles through the three regions and then rests in open awareness to see what the change is.

client exercise

Cellular Breathing

PURPOSE

Breath penetrates every cell and molecule of our bodies. It is the most direct method to feel our way into our basic health and well-being. Each cell in our bodies moves with breath. Allow yourself to imagine you are a single cell breathing and shifting with each breath movement. This exercise is a combination of imagining oneself as a cell breathing and sensing into the three-dimensionality of breath.

INSTRUCTIONS

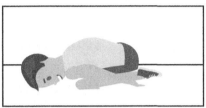

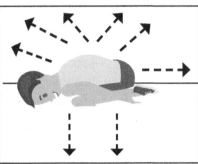

- Sense into the pain or challenge that you are working with. Visit this physical place briefly: Don't dwell, just note.
- Curl up into a ball, either by bending forward in a chair so your head is facing down, or by assuming a child's pose (like in yoga) on the floor. You can have your arms by your sides or rest your head on your forearms. Only go as far as your body allows. Watch for any discomfort and pain and make adjustments that fit your needs.
- Allow your belly to completely relax. Find your natural breath and connect with it in this position. Rest your body into gravity.
- Notice what this shape is doing to your breath already.
- Imagine yourself being a single cell. Imagine that your skin is permeable and soft and that the breath is now streaming through the skin. Your breath is becoming three-dimensional.
- Expand your breath into all directions outward from the center of your body.
- Imagine that your "cell" is filled with fluids and that you can move this fluidity each time you have the breath move.
- Notice the sense of weight and softness in your body.
- Gently sit up and sit in stillness, harvesting the effects of this exercise.

Reflection:

Can you re-visit your challenge or pain and see what it feels like from the more three-dimensional and fluid place? Are there any changes or new perceptions?

The image of my body now is: _____

The feeling in my body now is: _____

My pain/challenge feels: _____

client exercise

Deflating the Tire of Anxiety

PURPOSE

Imagine your stress as a tire that has too much air in it. Stress, tension and anxiety build up; it's difficult to contain or be with. You need to let out a little bit of "air" in order to take the pressure off. This exercise is doing just that: Exhaling the stress and anxiety out of the body.

INSTRUCTIONS

- Note the tensions in your body, even just briefly. It's difficult to stay with that awareness when you feel that pressure.
- Write or say out loud what your "hot zone" of tension is. Where is it located in the body?

  My "hot zone" is: _____

- Now count: One, two, three, four, five … exhale SLOWLY and imagine that tire, or "hot zone," deflating.
- Then inhale and count: Five, four, three, two, one. Send the inhale into the lower regions of your body: The lower belly and pelvis area. Fill the "base" of your body with the fresh and healthy inhale. This is your "neutral zone."

  My "neutral zone" is: _____

- You want to avoid placing the inhale and exhale into the same region of awareness.
- Exhale out from the area of challenge (your "hot zone") and inhale into the "neutral zone" of your body. If you happen to be working on a "hot zone" in your lower body, then choose a "neutral zone" somewhere else in the body. Perhaps it will be your lungs or the back of your body.

EXHALE SLOWLY: 1-2-3-4-5, out of the "hot zone"

INHALE slowly: 5-4-3-2-1, into the "neutral zone"

Lunar Breath - Diffusing the Tension

PURPOSE

The lunar breath is a soft and diffusing breath. It serves to melt tension in the body and regulate anxiety. This reminds the body to activate the parasympathetic response. Because the lunar breath is a very gentle breath and can be done internally, it's good for clients who feel self-conscious about breathing techniques in general. Encourage the client to close their eyes and listen to their own breath if they feel safe doing so.

INSTRUCTIONS

Part 1 – Building up to the lunar breath:

- Close your eyes.
- Make a "TH" sound. Your mouth should be open very slightly, the tip of your tongue lightly touching the back of your front teeth. Image the sound of a gentle wave rolling on the shore.
- It should be one long, sustained "TH" sound while exhaling. The inhale will come in naturally.
- The breath should be soft and long, focused on the sound.
- If needed, stay with this breath for a while.
- When you are comfortable with this part, add Part 2.

Part 2 – Lunar breath:

- Now, take this quality of the breath to the back of the throat.
- Close your mouth gently; no tension in the face.
- The "TH" sound should now move more to the back of the throat and out the nose. An image that might help is the sound of "wind in the trees," or "warm steam rising."
- Continue with long, sustained exhales. The inhales will fill in by themselves.
- You may experience a slight pressure in the throat while doing this exercise. If that is uncomfortable, you can either pause, do a few regular breaths, and then continue; or you can return to Part 1.
- The goal is to increase a sense of letting go gently and with control.
- Do this breath for at least three to four minutes to create a brain-state change.

Part 3 – Returning to the new baseline:

- Rest and return to normal breathing.
- What are you aware of right now?
- What is the quality of this breath that needs to happen right now?
- Look for a wave-like breath emerging in the chest and belly. Contact it when you see it. If it's not there, notice how much calmer you are. You may begin to yawn and get tired; that is the parasympathetic release.

CHAPTER 20
Working with Sound and Voice

Think of the human voice, the pitch, the tone and making sounds as the storyteller of your body. In the nuanced tone of a human voice we can detect joy, sadness, anger and more. We don't need to see. We can hear and sense the affective subtleties in the how we speak and sound. The voice has a tremendous healing capacity. Low pitches seem to relax the nervous system of the body; high pitches excite it.

Playing with sound into the body is a tool to stay present and inquire into the body. Studies have shown that even after a short time of singing or sounding, the level of immunoglobulin A (antibody) increases and creates a sense of well-being felt in the overall mood of the person. You can use sounding to work with your inner states, but also to discover who you are in a sound-story.

client exercise

Listening Bell

PURPOSE

This short, three-minute exercise serves to train the mind to focus its attention on a sound. The goal is to keep your attention solely focused on the sound, concentrating on how the sound fades and disappears with time.

This is a good exercise to teach stillness in a playful way when it is challenging to be mindful without distraction. Attention training cuts the distractions and heightens the sense of listening. It trains the client to focus on only one thing. This is good for clients who are easily distracted or can't focus well.

What you need:

Singing bowl, bells, or chimes. You can also you any chime apps on your phone.

INSTRUCTIONS

- Have a bell or singing bowl ready.

- Explain to your client the purpose of the exercise.

- Ask the client to notice the quiet before the sound starts, and then stop talking after the sound is rung.

- Have them close their eyes, take a breath and focus on the sound until it's completely gone.

- As the sound fades, ask them to notice what happens in their body; how stillness arrives. Ask: "What is present for you right now?" "What comes up for you as you sense the stillness?"

- You can encourage the client to use the sounds tool as way to stop the busy thoughts during the day.

Reflection:

My sounding body is:_____

The sounds that calm me are:_____

The sounds that wake me are:_____

client
exercise

Sounding into the Body

PURPOSE

The body is made up of 70%-80% fluids. Since sounds travel in fluids, we can use this body system to create resonating sounds for well-being. While any sounds can be used, accessible and pleasant sounds, such as forming vowel sounds, are the easiest to do. This practice of sound healing is an ancient practice that is done in many cultures. The benefit of sounding is to release anxiety and diffuse tension. Focusing on sounding can help elevate mood and alleviate negative thought patterns.

Sounding into the body is very helpful if a client can't do movements or feels restricted in some way. The gentle breath and vibrations of sounds carry subtle movements to the body without the client "moving" in an active way.

INSTRUCTIONS

- Place your hands gently on the area of your body you want to "send" your sound into. For training purposes, it is easiest to place your hand on your chest and make an "O" sound. You can feel the vibration in the chest.

- Make the sound soft and repeat it. Take in the softness of the sound and vibration. What do you notice?

- Next, try an "A" or "Ahh" sound into the chest. How is that sound different? Is the effect of that sound creating a different experience than the "O" sound?

- Repeat each sound three to four times, then return to your natural breath and notice your body mindfully.

- Don't push or exhaust your sound. As in any somatic practice, you want to be gentle and mindful of how your body receives the input. Follow what feels pleasurable and easy. The body will respond to this gentle sounding in its own way. The key is to be present to your experience.

- Once you feel comfortable with the sound, you can venture out and explore other sounds that come to you. It's important not to force the sounds. Take pleasure in the sounding experience.

- Repeat as needed.

client
exercise

"Hmmm" Sound

PURPOSE

The "Hmmm" sound is a very comforting sound. This is a beneficial sound when you feel anxious or depressed. Imagine "hmmm" being like how cats purr. We automatically say "hmmm" when we like an experience. It also resonates in the chest and produces a soothing effect. You can suggest using the sound when the client is agitated, anxious or has low energy. The low hum of the sound is gentle enough that it can be done by anyone without much effort. By practicing it in the office, you are rehearsing a tool that the client can do for themselves at home. The intention is to have a repertoire of sounds that are soothing and comforting and can be used with ease. This is a teaching for the client to practice self-kindness and gentleness to one's body.

INSTRUCTIONS

- "Hmmm," is a humming sound that you can do laying down or sitting up.

- Get into a comfortable position by reclining and rest the body completely.

- Send the "hmmm" sound into the chest region or belly region of your body. You can have one hand resting on the chest and feel the vibration of the sound into the chest region.

- Do two to three "hmmm" sounds and then wait and return to normal breathing.

- Repeat the two to three "hmmm" sounds and notice the effect they have. Imagine that you are sending the humming sound like a cat purring into your body. Follow the pleasure of this sound in your body. Where can you sense it? How do you notice the sound traveling inside your body?

This sound is very gentle and kind. You can do this before going to sleep or when you feel stressed. It's important not to force the sounds. Imagine the cat being touched and taking pleasure from the contact, purring in response. Repeat as needed.

Therapy session:

In the session, you can ask the client to do the sound and then notice its effects. Have the client study what happens in their body by asking: "Now what do you notice in your body?"

Follow up by asking: "If this sound had a message for you, what would it say?"

Message: _____

Corridor of Sound

client worksheet

PURPOSE

The voice can hold tension. Freeing the voice is another pathway into the somatic experience of the body. This exercise is a way to experiment using the voice as access to the body.

See what you "hold" in your voice or the expression of your voice. Notice what themes and emotions come up as you experiment with the voice. This exercise brings an element of play. Encourage experimenting and "making mistakes."

INSTRUCTIONS

- Examine how you view using your voice.

    My voice is:_____

    I believe that my voice or my sounds are: _____

- Close your eyes and imagine that your voice is on a slow elevator ride. Explore what it is like to express the up and down motion of this elevator through your voice.

- Start by going down in your voice, lowering the range. Then go up in your voice into a higher range. Do this up and down two to three times.

- Become mindful and notice your body and breath. How do you feel about your sound?

    My sound is: _____

    My voice feels: _____

    I want to express: _____

- Repeat the up and down scale of your voice. See if you can free yourself from the "right way" of doing this and experiment with how the voice can travel up and down the scale of your own range. Can you bring some fun and play into it?

Reflection:
- If your voice had a color, what would that be?
- If your voice had a shape, what would that be?
- What does your voice want to express?
- What have you been holding back?
- Before the sounding I feel_____ about my voice.

- After the sounding I feel_____ about my voice.
- Add a few comments about what you discover in your voice.

_____

_____

_____

CHAPTER 21
Working with Safe Touch

"Touch can have strong effects on our bodies, because when the skin is touched that stimulation is quickly transmitted to the brain, which in turn regulates our bodies. Depending on the type of touch we receive, we can either be calmed down or aroused."

-Tiffany Fields

WHY IS TOUCH IMPORTANT?

Touch is an essential human need. We are born and wired to connect through touch. Our most primal memories are connected with the kind of touch we received as infants and young children. Touching the skin can bring forth these memories. Touch can be soothing, a source of comfort. But it can also be a source of discomfort when the experience of touching was coupled with toxic touch, abuse, and trauma.

When working with touch in a therapeutic context, we need to be very clear about the ethical and legal requirements of our profession, as well as our therapeutic goals. It is often advised not to touch, due to legal and ethical concerns. Yet, safe, non-sexual and non-toxic touch can be immensely healing and restore self-soothing capacities.

Offering self-touch experiments that the client can do safely in the office or at home can be very beneficial to heal past touch traumas. By offering kind and clear boundaries, touch can be a therapeutic experience. This needs to be done with very clear and precise guidelines, and with an understanding of the impact of touch.

GENERAL THERAPEUTIC GUIDELINES

1. Educate yourself on the legal and ethical guidelines in your state and your profession.

2. Never touch without the consent of the client.

3. Sexual touch is **not** part of psychotherapy touch.

4. Examine the motivation for offering touch. If it serves you as the therapist, it is not a good motivation.

5. Safe touch means a clean, non-toxic, non-sexual touch. If there is any hesitation or question on your part, then don't touch.

6. Don't touch if there is any hesitation by the client, even if they consent. Track carefully for their response when you offer touch.

7. For a client with an abuse-touch history, use extra caution. Do a touch inventory and assessment to understand the client's history. Always be respectful and listen carefully if touch is invited and helpful.

8. Never rush touching experiments. Even suggesting touch is enough for the client to "study" their responses to touch. You might never touch the client, but rather work with the feelings and memories that get evoked by merely suggesting or exploring the possibility.

WHEN TO POTENTIALLY USE SAFE TOUCH

In general, there are four big categories for using touch:

1. To soothe and support strong feelings

2. To contain and ground when working with fear, anxiety and dissociation

3. To know safe body boundaries, particularly when exploring safety

4. To study memories or feelings attached to touch

TIPS FOR USING TOUCH

1. Ask permission: "Is it okay to touch you right now?"

2. Be specific: "Is it okay to touch you on your right shoulder right now?"

3. Be mindful and deliberate, with a clear objective: "I can see how upset you are. Is it okay to touch you on your shoulder?"

4. Make sure you touch where you agreed and don't move your hand around. That is unsafe and unpredictable. Be very specific.

5. Use a gentle and listening kind of touch: Once the client shifts and the objective is done (e.g., they've stopped crying and are sitting up), remove your hand and establish the right distance again.

6. Debrief how the touch was experienced by the client. Encourage honest feedback. Listen carefully and make adjustments for the future. If they say it was just "okay," perhaps it was not needed after all.

7. Track for transference and countertransference. Touch is a strong bonding experience. Don't overuse it or make that a default mode for every time the client has a strong feeling.

client
exercise

Self-Touch - Tapping

PURPOSE

When you self-touch, you are waking up the skin and increasing sensations in the body. Self-touch can help you experience yourself directly and feel into your body boundary.

Tapping helps you sense yourself as "here" rather than "there." It is also a soothing and comforting motion that helps you regulate yourself.

INSTRUCTIONS

This exercise can be done standing or sitting.

- Cup one hand slightly so your palm and fingers can gently pat or tap parts of the body.
- Rhythmically and gently tap your opposite arm from the wrist to the shoulder. Switch hands and do the other arm.
- Move on to your legs and go from the ankle to the thigh of each leg. You can engage each leg with both hands as you tap down, as if you are tap-hugging each leg. You can also choose to do both legs at the same time. Keep a steady rhythm going.
- Next move to the back. Slightly bend forward so you can reach the kidney area and the lower back. Make sure you don't tap directly on the spine.
- Then move to the front of the body. Start with the chest, by moving from the shoulder joint into the center of the chest with one hand. Repeat three times. Then switch hands and move from the other shoulder into the center of the chest.
- Now tap the belly in a clock-wise direction. Make sure you are gentle as you tap the organs.
- Move to the soles of the feet. You can do one or both at the same time.
- Lastly, move from the crown of the head to the back of the neck. For the face, you want to open your hands and tap with your fingers.
- Sit quietly for a moment and sense your body after the tapping.

Reflection:

- What do you notice in your body right now?
- What is most alive?
- What area is numb or not accessible right now?
- Describe your overall body awareness: _____

client exercise

Cueing Hands

PURPOSE

Placing your hands on your body is a cueing of attention. By touching your own body with intention, awareness, and focus, you are directing attention towards the area of inquiry. This works well if you have an area of tension or discomfort, or have a place in the body that you want to learn more about.

When you place your hands, make sure your touch is gentle, kind, and open. The best way to touch an area of your body is to slowly place your hand and "cup" the area. For example, you can cup your tight jaws by placing your hands around the face and jaw. Or you can cup your hands around a tense arm or leg. Quality of touch matters: by doing this slowly and softly, you will experience more heightened sensations and information.

Be receptive and inquisitive. It's important to wait and be with the touch so you can drop into your experience. Notice your breath and "send your breath" to the area of your touch. You should feel a change in your tissue, tension, or level of discomfort in a few minutes. Be patient and wait for your body!

INSTRUCTIONS

- Identify an area of the body that needs attention.

- Slow down and notice that area first.

- Slowly place your hand on that area. Make sure your touch is soft, slow and receptive, as if you are "listening with your hands."

- Stay with your touch and be present to what your experience is as you are self-touching.

- Now breathe slowly and consciously into this area. "Send" your breath into the place you are working on. It can help to imagine the breath traveling to the area and the area being receptive to it.

- Stay mindful and inquisitive.

- Are you noticing any change? Is the tension lessening?

client exercise

Compassionate Self-Touch

PURPOSE

This tool encourages the client to feel into what kind of compassionate touch is needed. It sensitizes the client to what kind of touch is nourishing and safe. This is beneficial to facilitate self-kindness or when restoring negative experiences from past touch.

This practice can be done sitting, standing or laying down. Encourage the client to slow down and be mindful. Be aware that self-touch can be triggering and bring forth deep feelings and memories. You want to track for these sensitivities and reinforce the self-kindness. Stopping and noticing helps regulate any intensity that may arise.

This tool is to facilitate letting go of negative experiences around touch and to safely feel touch as a positive experience. Emphasize the self-compassion.

INSTRUCTIONS

- Have a set-up inquiry about what it means to have a compassionate self-touch. Ask: "What does compassionate self-touch mean to you?" "What would the quality of this touch be?"

  Answer: _____

- Tune into your body and notice. "What area of your body would like to receive your own touch?" (Note: encourage easy areas, such as arms, hands, chest, face.)

  Answer: _____

- Now tune into the part of yourself that knows how to be compassionate. "What is that part?" "If it had a personality or an image associated with it, what would that be?"

  Answer: _____

- Invite the client to very slowly touch the area they want to work with. You can say: "Go ahead, slowly reach toward the _____ and let your hand touch your _____ right now."

  Critical: "Notice HOW your _____ is receiving the touch right now. Stay here and notice."

  Answer: _____

- "Stay here as long as you need. Let yourself take in the _____ (warmth, kindness, softness—any quality the client identified in Question #1)."

- When they are finished, ask them to slowly remove their touch and study what the impact of that kind of touch is right now.

  Right now I am noticing: _____

SOMATIC TOOLS FOR STRESS AND TRAUMA

CHAPTER 22
Trauma and the Body

"Many people who don't know a lot about trauma think that trauma has something to do with something that happened to you a long time ago. In fact, the past is the past and the only thing that matters is what happens right now. And what is trauma is the residue that a past event leaves in your own sensory experiences in your body and it's not that event out there that becomes intolerable but the physical sensations with which you live that become intolerable and you will do anything to make them go away."

— Bessel van der Kolk

POLYVAGAL THEORY: A VERY BRIEF OVERVIEW

The Polyvagal Theory of Dr. Stephen Porges describes three main stages of human and other mammal autonomic development. When we are feeling safe, we want to connect and engage with others. When we are feeling threatened, we mobilize to meet the danger with a fight or flight response. When we are overwhelmed by threat, we survive by immobilizing or shutting down our autonomic nervous system.

The autonomic nervous system (ANS) regulates internal organ function and responds to threat. The ANS has two branches: the sympathetic branch and the parasympathetic branch. Both are needed to regulate our nervous system. The sympathetic branch activates the body into fight or flight in threat situations. The parasympathetic branch calms the body and controls digestion. The interplay between the two makes up the resilient ANS and helps with self-regulating capacities when one is under stress.

Dr. Porges has identified the vagus nerve as playing a central role in regulating the gut (viscera), breath and heart rate. 80% of the vagus nerve fibers send signals to the brain about the viscera, which is our gut response. This nerve also controls the muscles of the face, heart and lungs, and is responsible when we engage with other human beings. When we are in a safe social engagement, the vagus nerve down-regulates and calms the sympathetic nervous branch. In this situation, we are able to handle minor stressors as we find the company of others soothing.

- When you feel safe: You want to play and connect = Social Engagement Capacity

- When you feel threatened and in danger: You want to get away or be aggressive = Primitive survival responses such as flight or fight

- When you feel a life threat or terror and you can't get away or defend: You want to wait until the threat has passed = Your body freezes to stay safe

The following exercises will help clients get in touch with their own nervous system and learn when and how to engage the sympathetic and parasympathetic branches for energy, calm, safety, and connection.

client worksheet

Tracking Your Own Nervous System

PURPOSE

This tool allows you to learn about how and what you can do to increase your sense of safety, get connected, and learn to calm or to engage with activity.

INSTRUCTIONS

Use the chart below to track and learn about your client's nervous system. By engaging your nervous system, you can teach it to help you to become more engaged, calm or active.

- The Social Engagement System is activated by talking to a trusted friend, spending time with a beloved pet, or doing activities that make you feel safe.
- The Sympathetic System engages when you are playful and active, such as moving your body to music, playing sports, journaling your thoughts, or stretching your body.
- The Parasympathetic System activates when you listen to soothing music, practice conscious breathing, receive a nourishing touch, hear a pleasant voice, etc.

Social Engagement	Sympathetic	Parasympathetic
What makes you feel connected?	What makes you feel active?	What makes you feel calm?
How do you reach out? What works?	How do you support your engagement with others?	How can you create healthy habits to train your calm state?

client worksheet

Expanded Window of Tolerance Chart

PURPOSE

The Window of Tolerance Chart is a visual aid to help the client identify when they are in aroused zones and when they are in resilient zones.

There are three main zones: Hyper-arousal, Optimum Arousal Zone (OAZ), and Hypo-arousal.

The optimum zone of arousal is where the client can experience stress and is able to handle it with ordinary coping strategies.

When the stress becomes unmanageable, the client might spike into the hyper-arousal zone or drop into the hypo-arousal zone. In these arousal zones, the client is using coping mechanisms that are based more on survival, such as fleeing, fighting or freezing. Hyper-arousal can be subtle at first, such as irritation. A hyper-aroused response indicates they are up on the chart and outside what is optimum. The same is true if the client becomes withdrawn and stiff, indicating the beginning of hypo-arousal and potentially going towards a freezing response.

Once the client goes outside the OAZ, responses become reactions, the polyvagal system becomes activated, and resiliency will be compromised. This can result in having negative stress reactions, triggered memories, and trauma symptoms.

INSTRUCTIONS

Use the colored graph to psycho-educate your client on the different zones. You want to highlight that the Optimum Arousal Zone is the preferred zone to heal stress and trauma symptoms. You want to stay in the OAZ when working to heal symptoms, and work towards that zone when dealing with symptoms. Highlight that the OAZ is a fluid zone, that the fluctuations are the building of a resilient nervous system.

Use general terms to describe the zones with this approach: "You might find when you are in the hyper-arousal zone that you experience anxiety, fear, worry, irritability and anger. What have you found?" Ask the client to fill in their experience. Or when talking about the hypo-arousal zone you can say: "You may have noticed feelings of depression, numbness, frozenness, and being withdrawn. How do you experience this zone?"

Teach your client to be aware of how they travel to the different zones. This will help them start to become cognizant of what their triggers are. When triggers are identified, it will be easier to work towards what needs to heal.

The expanded zone is the region of the impulses that are triggered under stress, but can be changed or influenced with mindfulness, breath and body awareness.

Below are some inquiry questions you can utilize to help your client gain more awareness and also learn when to apply tools for changing their level of arousal.

Reflection:

Chart the zones in your own words:

In the hypo-arousal zone:

I am aware that:_____

I notice in my body:_____

My thoughts are:_____

My impulses are:_____

I want to instinctively do/be:_____

When stressed, I :_____

In the expanded zone, I can use (technique/tool)_____to change my triggers.

In the hyper-arousal zone:

I am aware that:_____

I notice in my body:_____

My thoughts are:_____

My impulses are:_____

I want to instinctively do/be:_____

When stressed, I :_____

In the expanded zone, I can use (technique/tool)_____to change my triggers.

In the zone of optimum arousal:

I am aware that:_____

When I experience stress, I notice:_____

My body feels:_____

My impulses are:_____

My strength is:_____

I am able to:_____

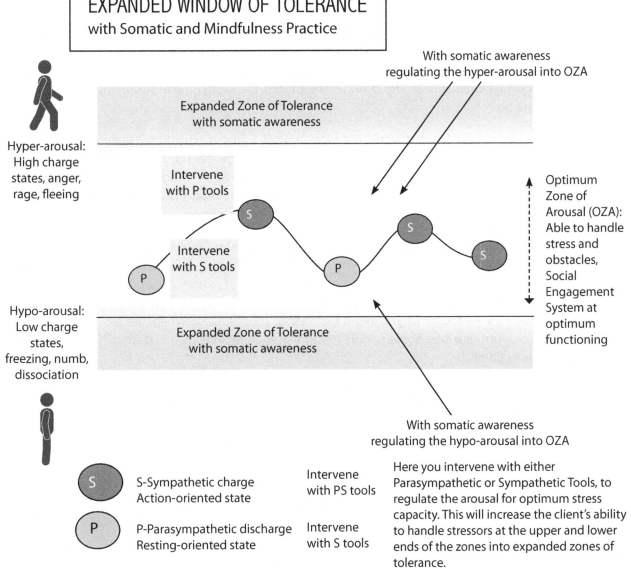

EXPANDED WINDOW OF TOLERANCE
with Somatic and Mindfulness Practice

With somatic awareness regulating the hyper-arousal into OZA

Expanded Zone of Tolerance with somatic awareness

Hyper-arousal: High charge states, anger, rage, fleeing

Intervene with P tools

Intervene with S tools

Optimum Zone of Arousal (OZA): Able to handle stress and obstacles, Social Engagement System at optimum functioning

Hypo-arousal: Low charge states, freezing, numb, dissociation

Expanded Zone of Tolerance with somatic awareness

With somatic awareness regulating the hypo-arousal into OZA

S-Sympathetic charge Action-oriented state

Intervene with PS tools

P-Parasympathetic discharge Resting-oriented state

Intervene with S tools

Here you intervene with either Parasympathetic or Sympathetic Tools, to regulate the arousal for optimum stress capacity. This will increase the client's ability to handle stressors at the upper and lower ends of the zones into expanded zones of tolerance.

client exercise

How Can I Resource Myself?

PURPOSE

Learning to identify what your resources are is critical in helping your stress and trauma symptoms. First you identify what triggers you into stress and trauma responses. Then, you reflect and experiment with what could resource you. The charts on the next page invite you to indicate what your triggers are and what connections you can find to resource yourself.

INSTRUCTIONS

- On the next page reflect on the triggers you experience and where you would place them on the chart of the arousal continuum. Hyper-arousal triggers, for example, are excessive worry, anxiety or anger. Hypo-arousal triggers can be emotional withdrawal or feeling frozen by fear. The stronger the trigger, the higher the arousal. Note the trigger in the box.

- Now think about what would help you in these times of activation. What would ease your response to the triggers? What would help when a trigger puts you into an arousal zone? What are the resources you can identify in response to the trigger? For example, for some a resource might be remembering a kind word, breathing calmly, or moving the body and not feeling frozen. Resources are unique to each person.

- What triggers and experiences belong in the Optimum Arousal Zone? How do you handle them? What resources you here? You might notice breathing can help you handle small stressors. When you are in the higher and lower arousal zones this may not work anymore. For example, when you are in the OAZ, you have a sense of strength, optimism even if life is tough. Or you might experience your arousal as manageable, not frozen nor highly anxious. Some people report in this zone of being a in state of health, or flow or wellbeing.

- Make sure that you reflect on "how" you are helped in the bottom reflection box. You want to spend some time thinking about how you get from arousal to resource so you can learn to take charge of your triggers. Make a commitment to practicing your resources that help you feel self-regulated, grounded and within the Optimum Zone of Arousal. The more you practice your resource tools the more you are able to expand you OAZ. This means that when stressors come your way you don't habitually respond with hyper or hypo arousal symptoms, but rather feel in control and calm.

How Can I Resource Myself?

Use the instructions on the previous page to fill out the following charts. Use an "O" for each resource and a "X" for each trigger. Once you marked them all, take a moment and sit back and reflect on the O's and X's on your chart. Then draw a connecting line between them and reflect on how you can get from a trigger to a resource. What helps you transform the triggers?

EXAMPLE: I am aware that:_____I freeze when I am yelled at_____.

Hyper-arousal Zone (HyperZ)

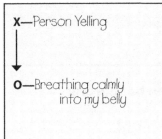

X—Person Yelling

O—Breathing calmly into my belly

My Triggers are:
Angry person yelling on phone

My resources are:
Disengage with the person and belly breathe

I get there by:
Remembering to breathe and not taking the angry person personally

Optimum Zone of Arousal (OZA)

I feel in my power, connected with myself and able to handle stuff

My Triggers are:
Work stress that is not too much

My resources are:
Planning ahead and anticipating the tense work environment. Communicate better with the "angry" people at work, so they don't ambush me.

I get there by:
Write clear emails, don't procrastinate and wait for them to blow up at me.

Hypo-Arousal Zone (HypoZ)

X— I wait and procrastinate

O—I get lethargic and hopeless

My Triggers are:
Angry person that is not expressing it, but I can feel it, and it makes me freeze up. Walk on egg shells around them.

My resources are:
My family and friends that love me. I remember them in that moment.

I get there by:
I look and turn my head towards the pictures that are my resources. I counter the fear moment with calling up my family and friends that love me. Makes me breathe easier.

Hyper-arousal Zone (HyperZ)

	My Triggers are: **My resources are:** **I get there by:**

Optimum Zone of Arousal (OZA)

	Triggers I can handle are: **My resources that work are:** **I get there by:**

Hypo-Arousal Zone (HypoZ)

	My Triggers are: **My resources are:** **I get there by:**

REFLECTION

_____

_____

_____

_____

_____

_____

How did you get from an activated place to your resource?

_____

_____

_____

Next step is to make a mindful and conscious effort to reacting the resources that work. List the three top resources that are your go to:

_____

_____

_____

NOTING MY ACTIVATION TRIGGERS

Note what your external vs. internal triggers are. This will help you identify what comes from external stimuli and what you can possibly do to work with that. For example, avoid or anticipate? What are your internal triggers? Do you have repetitive thoughts, images? Can you bring other internal resources to soothe the inner triggers?

External events that triggered me today:

_____

_____

_____

Inner experiences that triggered me today?

_____

_____

_____

External trigger helpers:

_____

_____

_____

Internal trigger helpers

_____

_____

_____

client worksheet

Scanning Towards Safety

PURPOSE

This tool will help you learn how to move towards internalized safety.

Instinctively, we use our eyes to scan for safety. When entering a new situation, we search for visual cues to confirm that we are safe or that we need to somehow tend to safety. Being safe is primal and fundamental to thriving. By consciously using the scanning by our eyes, we can begin to create an embodied sense of safety—we are actively taking care of making the situation safe.

Stress and trauma experiences can compromise the natural sense of safety and put us on high alert. Being aware of looking with intention and scanning provides a way to start slowing down the activations in the body. Look for cues such as calming of the breath, curiosity about the surroundings, or an overall sense of ease as you scan. You want to work to reduce any vigilance and increase the sense of safety in the body.

INSTRUCTIONS

Use the chart below to track your eye movements and record your body sensations. It is important to slow down the eye movement and chart every time there is a sensation in the body. Move back and forth between scanning the eyes across the room, noticing the sensations in the body, and charting. Make sure you look up for scanning the room and then chart.

Scan the room; move your eyes.

Rest your eyes on one point and notice your body. Write down what you sense and feel.

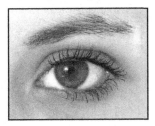

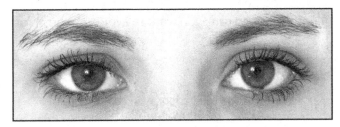

#1 Scan – – – – – – – – – – – ➔ I sense:_____

#2 Scan – – – – – – – – – – – ➔ I feel in my body:_____

#3 Scan – – – – – – – – – – – ➔ I notice a change in: _____

What changes in your body and your sense of safety?

_____

MOVE!

client
exercise

PURPOSE

When you start freezing into hypo-arousal or spinning-out with hyper-arousal, the antidote is easy: MOVE! That means whatever you are doing, wherever you are, when you notice the signs of freezing, when your body is feeling overcome with anxiety, you need to MOVE! It's easy to do, but hard to remember. This is a very directive instruction. You can practice this in the office with your therapist and then internalize the voice that says "move" when you need it.

Moving means anything from getting up and walking across the room to putting on music and dancing. You can shake your arms around, jump—whatever you feel safe and comfortable doing where you are. If you are in a situation where you feel self-conscious, excuse yourself to leave the room and use the opportunity to MOVE. No one will notice. The main point is that you don't give in to the frozen or anxious feeling in your body. As soon as you feel it: MOVE. That way you are training yourself to interrupt this pattern.

Note to therapist:

You can train this response in the office by practicing "move." Agree with the client when to say the word and have them practice getting up and walking around. Encourage a quick pace. This is a very directive instruction; make sure you talk to your client about what kind of voice they want to hear. It needs to be a strong command, but not harsh or jarring in any way. Rehearse with the client what tone of voice would work for them. The goal is for them to remember this word when they find themselves freezing or spinning-out. The "move" word serves to interrupt and mobilize the ancient defense system of the body—the client is able to move around and not feel stuck or overwhelmed. In that moment, they have gained their agency again. Make sure your rehearsal is done with mindfulness and care; you want to avoid coming across like a commander.

INSTRUCTIONS

- Cut out the MOVE icons on the next page.

- Place them strategically in areas where you often notice freezing or spinning-out. Is it near the phone after talking to people? By the computer? Think about where you can put these icons. They are instructions for you to look at when you notice freezing or spinning-out.

- You can practice this MOVE activity without being activated. When you see the icons, move around, walk, pace, dance. You are training your own response time for that moment when freezing or spinning-out overtakes you.

Rate yourself before and after the MOVE instruction.

Before I move, on a scale of 1-10 I feel (please circle):

1   2   3   4   5   6   7   8   9   10

Thoughts:_____

After I move, on a scale 1-10 I feel (please circle):

1   2   3   4   5   6   7   8   9   10

Thoughts:_____

MOVE NOW	MOVE NOW	MOVE NOW

Imagine Running Faster Than the Tiger

PURPOSE

This exercise uses your imagination. Visualizing outrunning a tiger connects you with your actual body movements. By imagining yourself as running like a tiger (or any fast-moving animal), you are triggering a set of neurons in the brain helping you to connect with ancient fleeing impulses in the body. You might feel some twitching in the legs or arms or an actual impulse to run as you imagine yourself outrunning a fast-moving animal.

When you engage with this fleeing response of the body in a mindful way, the body is reminded of this ancient brain and body connection. This is useful in helping re-negotiate trauma responses such as feeling immobile and frozen. Please use mindful attention as you imagine this scenario. You can stop anytime and notice any changes that feel empowering and helpful. Avoid any overwhelm or more frozenness.

Since trauma can interrupt our sense of self-agency, this tool can be helpful in gaining back some power. Animals that represent strength and speed can be useful to imagine. Feel free to substitute the tiger image for any image that the client associates with speed and strength.

Running connects anyone with the defensive impulse of fleeing. But if running was impossible due to an inescapable situation, it's important to reconnect with that cut-off impulse. This can be done through imagery, then through actual muscle impulse. Track for motor impulses such as twitching in the leg. Connect the body awareness with the impulses and allow for small, deliberate movement while imagining a successful escape or running. The focus is on connecting imagery and impulse, and a successful completion of the movement.

INSTRUCTIONS

- Close your eyes and call up the image of running. If it helps, you can imagine running faster than a tiger (or substitute any fast-running animal). **Avoid calling up the actual traumatic memory**, but work with the impulse of running as a somatic event—not a trauma recovery process.
- Imagine the impulse to run. Visualize yourself escaping and running. Notice what pace you are running. What else happens as you run? How do you breathe?

Note to therapist:

Track for body twitches and other impulses. Keep bringing the focus to the actual running to complete the action of the movement. Gently remind the client to keep the image of running together with the impulses. Make sure you slow the client down so they can be fully present in this experience. Avoid any emotional overwhelm. This is not to process any trauma memory, but to help the client feel a sense of self-agency in the body. Look for strength, power and confidence. Pause or stop when the client is getting stiff, frozen or overwhelmed; you do not want to re-enact any previous trauma experience.

Reflection:

- Running, I imagine_____

- I outran the "tiger of"_____(name the reason for your running)

- I beat the tiger and feel_____

client
exercise

The Container Principle

PURPOSE

The way we perceive trauma and the beliefs we form due to the trauma are both factors in resolving the symptoms. A common perception is that "time will heal," but the beliefs that get created are often not taken into account in the process. The images below will aid in psycho-educating your client on their perception of their trauma and will provide a starting inquiry into what beliefs your client holds.

A common belief is that as time passes, the trauma will shrink. What is more truthful is that the more resource the person develops over time, the more capable they become to deal with their trauma. Their "container" becomes bigger and therefore absorbs the trauma experience better. The experiences that resources provide become larger and will re-calibrate the original stress and trauma experiences. Thus, the importance of building resources in aiding the healing process.

Use the worksheets on pages 224 and 225 to reflect on the resources and capacities that can be built over time. Reflect on the beliefs that are held around "what heals."

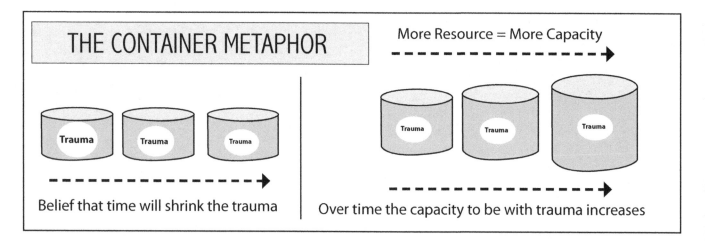

INSTRUCTIONS

Use the images above to show your clients the different ways we can view the trauma experience.

Discuss the container principle and what kind of resources can be built to help re-calibrate responses to stress and trauma. Then have your client reflect on their personal beliefs surrounding the healing of trauma.

Step 1: Inquiry into the beliefs

- What do you believe about your trauma experience?
- How did you come to that belief about what happened to you?
- How do you view the trauma currently?

- What are the messages you received about your trauma? Identify them and write them down.
- What do you believe your body can "take" in regards to your trauma? (E.g. "I believe that there is a limit," "My body can't process it," "My body will process the trauma somehow," "Time will heal.")

Step 2: Inquiry into the change of beliefs

- How would you like to change your beliefs?
- If you were a container that changed over time, how would the container need to change?
- What would the first step be towards this?
- How can you develop the necessary resources?
- Identify the resources you currently have that help you deal with the trauma symptoms.

Step 3: Worksheets

Have the client journal, reflect on, and discuss their beliefs with you. Use the following worksheets to assess their current state of beliefs. Because beliefs change over time, continue to use these worksheets regularly to update any changing beliefs and help the client reflect on, and chart, their progress.

The Container Metaphor Beliefs

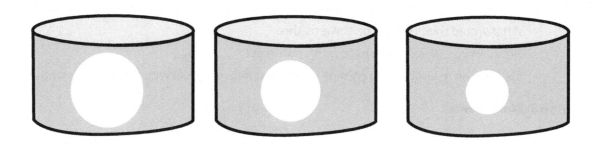

WHAT DO YOU BELIEVE ABOUT YOUR TRAUMA EXPERIENCE?

I believe... _____

_____

_____

_____

_____

_____

_____

_____

_____

_____

_____

_____

_____

_____

The Container Metaphor Resources

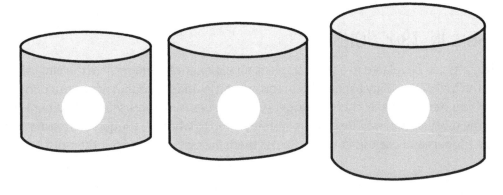

My resources are… _____

_____

_____

_____

_____

- -

I will develop… _____

_____

_____

_____

_____

_____

client
worksheet

Tracking Triggers Chart

PURPOSE & INSTRUCTIONS

Triggers can be related to a set of unpleasant experiences. Triggers are the early alarm system of the body. The ability to chart them can aid you in understanding what your body is trying to tell you. Keep a weekly chart of triggers you observe. Allow yourself to document the triggers in the most neutral way. Be curious and stay open to what the triggers are teaching you. Chart the triggers and use this chart to discuss them in sessions with your therapist.

What kind of trigger?	When? (Day/Time)	What happened? (Event)	How intense? 1-10 Scale (10 = most intense)	Where in the body? Familiar?	What did you do at that moment?	What did you learn? Anything you did to prompt the trigger?	Notes

therapist worksheet

Trauma Stressor Timeline

Name of Client:_____

DOB:_____

Date Treatment Started:_____

Timeline Completed:_____

In year segments, please list the traumas and stressors your client has experienced.

Age	Trauma Event	Main Issues Unresolved
Prenatal		
0-5		
6-10		
11-15		
16-20		
21-25		
26-30		
31-35		
36-40		
41-45		
46-50		
51-60		
61-70		
70+		

client
exercise

Shaking to Safety

PURPOSE

Body tremors are a common symptom associated with anxiety and fear. The body's flight, fight, freeze system is designed to help the body react quickly and efficiently during duress and threat. Once the threat has subsided, the body uses the shaking movement to process the threat and restore its equilibrium. Body tremors occur naturally during the stress response of hyper-stimulation. The amount of stress can't be fully processed and the body seeks relief. This nervous system activity is often experienced as an involuntary response, but we can use this natural system in a conscious way by gently initiating this movement to entice the body towards relaxation and restoration.

Shakes come in waves and can vary in intensity. This exercise purposefully allows shaking, and directing the shaking, so you can experience a release and restoration. This is especially helpful after you have worked with a challenging client, or are feeling vulnerable after an activating session where you feel anxiety or are triggered. Allow at least 15 minutes for this so you can taper down the shaking to a calm and restful place.

You can use these instructions with your client as well, guiding them gently through the same process. There are proven trauma-release techniques that use this process to work with fear and PTSD symptoms, demonstrating how to overcome the dominating grip of fear. To learn more, please consult the work of Dr. David Berceli and TRE techniques and Somatic Experiencing.

A word of caution:

Too much shaking that does not go towards restoration of equilibrium can be emotionally activating, resulting in the opposite effect. You are looking to promote a safe release in the body, not activation and more anxiety. It's important to pause and notice, and not just shake for a long time. You want to bring mindfulness to the shaking, not just shake without any awareness—which can lead to feeling overwhelmed and more anxious. If you notice this is not being beneficial, stop.

INSTRUCTIONS

Take 15 minutes for this exercise. Each phase is about five minutes.

There are three phases: 1. Evoking   2. Moving Through   3. Cooling Down

Do this exercise standing. Have your stance wide so you feel supported by your legs. Close your eyes if you are comfortable; you want to see your body from the inside.

1. Evoking

- Notice your body standing and tune into your physical spine.

- Let your arms hang by your sides; your head will be moving along with the rhythm you initiate.
- Begin to gently move your legs rhythmically up and down, bending them slightly. This results in a gentle, wave-like motion through the spine.
- Start with a gentle and rhythmic shake that feels comfortable to your body.
- Allow this movement to be the same rhythm the whole time until it becomes second nature and you don't think of "doing the movement."

2. Moving Through

- In this second phase, you might notice how the body is moving by itself. You are not thinking about the movement anymore; just allowing it to move you.
- There might be feelings such as sadness, grief or anxiety floating through. Allow them to be there without amplifying them.
- The rhythm of the movement is how you can process through the body. The body will remember how to do this for you.
- Trust the movement.
- Let the body shake be even and rhythmic, allowing whatever comes up here. The more relaxed you can be in your body, the better.

3. Cooling Down

- There is a natural winding down as you listen to your body.
- Slow the movement down, making it gradually smaller.
- You might notice a release in your body, small tremors, an emotion, or sensations that feel good or pleasurable.
- You want to initiate the body into the cooling-down phase to rest.
- Let the body come to a standstill and notice what is there.
- There are often small inner shakes that release, and you want to be present for that.
- Stand firm and still and notice the waves of release subsiding.
- Once you feel clear and calm, or a shift in the activation, end the exercise.

Before, after and in the session:

You can use this technique most effectively before and after the session. During a session, this would be distracting for your client. If you feel nervous about a client, you might take your time preparing for this session and work with your anxiety by using the shaking technique.

After a session that was emotionally charged or triggering, you can use this as well so you don't bring your work home. This is an excellent self-care tool to restore your nervous system before you leave your office for the day.

If you find yourself triggered during a session, you can allow for small shakes that are naturally occurring, but be mindful that your attention will be drawn away from your client—you don't want this to be hindering your work.

client
exercise

Orienting Gong Awareness

PURPOSE

Every experience is transient and moves on. Just like the fading sound of a gong, your trauma experience can fade as well. Listen to the gong once as pure sound fading. The second time visualize your image or story fading with the sound.

What you will need:

A bell, gong, or a gong app

INSTRUCTIONS

- Sit quietly and observe the room.
- Study each detail. Pay attention to any changes in your breathing; notice any changes in your attention.
- Close your eyes and examine your experience.
- As the gong rings once, examine your reaction to the sound and its effect. Allow the sound to resonate until it completely fades and is gone.
- Examine how you orient to the sound. What happens inside your body?
- Can you follow the sound fading? What changes can you detect in your breathing?
- When you open your eyes, what happens to your focus and concentration?
- Ring the gong a second time. Now imagine your activation, or story, melts with the fading of the sound.
- Connect with the sound and your breath at the same time. Repeat two to three times.

client worksheet

Calling Your Experience by Its True Name

PURPOSE

This tool helps you gain awareness and clarity of your experience. Learning to name what is happening is the first step towards making a change. Naming the present moment is an excellent tool when you feel hypo-aroused. This helps you ground, become more present and less activated. Use your perceptions to feel and sense.

INSTRUCTIONS

Learning how to differentiate between what has activated you and what is actually happening is useful when learning to distance and regulate your feelings. This worksheet can be used in the session or as homework after a session.

Right now I am feeling _____ (emotion) **and I am sensing in my body**_____, _____, _____ (at least 3 body sensations)**, because I am remembering** _____ (name the trauma by title only, no details!).

At the same time, I am looking around where I am now in _____ (name your surrounding, such as "my living room," etc.).

I am looking around and I see _____ (the place where I am at in this moment; turn your head and take in the details of what you see).

What I mostly notice is_____ (describe some of the things you see now in this place).

And in this moment I know _____ (title of trauma only) **is not happening now/anymore.**

I am here!

Make a statement that declares your present-moment state:

I am/feel_____

Releasing the Psoas Muscle

PURPOSE

The psoas muscle is an important muscle in the body. It is also referred to as the fight or flight muscle when one is under stress or threat. We use the psoas muscle to get away or contract. Chronic stress or trauma can tighten this muscle and create pain in the groin or lower back area.

Learning to release the psoas muscle can aid in trauma recovery, as well as trauma memory release. This exercise focuses on a passive release of the psoas muscle.

INSTRUCTIONS

There are two passive ways to work with the psoas muscle: One is against the wall and the other is with the feet on the ground.

Option 1 - Feet on the ground:

- Lay on your back with your feet flat on the ground. Make sure you're comfortable.

- Connect with your breath and the surface beneath you.

- Begin to gently lift your feet as if they are sliding out of water. This should be a very slow movement of lifting that takes no effort.

- Then place your feet back on the ground.

- Make sure you are NOT lifting from the psoas muscle, but rather from the big thighbone.

- This might take a little practice.

Option 2 - Feet up on the wall:

- Lay on your back. Make sure you're comfortable.

- Connect with your breath and the surface beneath you.

- Place your feet up on the wall in a 90-degree angle.

- Working on one leg at a time, release the psoas muscle by sliding the leg towards the hips, as if you are letting the leg fall. This creates a passive movement in the psoas muscle. Make sure you are not guiding the movement to the hip, but simply letting the leg fall.

- Do this action four to five times, then repeat this process with the other leg.

CHAPTER 23
Somatic Resourcing

SOMATIC RESOURCES - THRIVING RESOURCES

A somatic resource is anything that creates a sense of calm and psycho-physical stability in the internal state of the trauma client—from a helpful memory to an internalized body awareness. A somatic resource becomes a refuge from the ongoing stimulus that life brings through the eyes of the trauma client. This gives one not just a means for survival, but a pathway towards a more fruitful and thriving life.

Survival Resources

- Survival resources are the flight-fight-flee responses of our bodies. They are effective for survival because they help us to cope under stressful and traumatic circumstances. When we can't take anymore stimulation, we turn to survival resources. However, these are not useful if used repeatedly. Survival resources are beyond cognition; they are the body's answer to severe stress and overwhelm.

Somatic and Thriving Resources

- Somatic and thriving resources help us to live to our full potential. They are the capacity to think, feel, sense and relate without activation or overwhelm. Somatic resources help rebuild and restore us to thriving and balanced lives. These resources allow us to stay with intensity and grow further, learn, and adapt without the damage to our bodies and nervous systems.

Some of the key somatic and thriving resources that have been examined include:

1. Grounding exercises: Actively moving and connecting feet and legs to the ground beneath in a psycho-somatic way.

2. Earth connection: A physical sense of belonging to the earth. This can be done by standing and feeling your feet on the ground, walking with awareness of the ground beneath you, or connecting with the idea that you are held up by the earth.

3. Walking with awareness in the body. This can be a simple walk in the neighborhood.

4. Working actively with the psoas muscle (the big fight or flight muscle): Use release techniques for easing the tension of the psoas.

5. Compassionate self-touch. Explore what kind of touch feels good to you. Experiment with gentle patting self-touch.

6. Therapist touch, when appropriate, safe and non-sexual. Touch needs to be provided with great care and attention to boundaries. Please consult your regional laws and ethics on this subject, or refer to a qualified body worker.

7. Sensory awareness: Simple noticing of the body as a practice. For example, you can sit in the sunshine and sense the rays on your skin.

8. Movement of body-expression, such as gentle movements and dance. Find out what movements feel right to you. Large dance movements or small intrinsic ones?

9. Working with pain: Renegotiating the sensory intensity through micro-movements and breath.

10. Breath exercises that enhance well-being. Increase your capacity for breath intake and exhale. Be playful and experiment with breath practices that feel good to you.

11. Mindfulness practices that engage the physical body.

12. Creative expressions such as art and writing, making or listening to music.

13. Nature: You can take walks in nature or use your imagination to visualize nature.

14. Physical exercise: Any exercise that creates a sense of well-being. Find out what helps you.

15. Visualizing in your mind a safe space to be.

CULTIVATING DUAL AWARENESS

In normal consciousness, we are able to strike a balance between the many internal and external sensory stimuli that occupy our awareness at any one time. We can shift from one to the other: Coordinating, synthesizing, negotiating, and interpreting. Individuals with PTSD, however, become habituated to paying an inordinate amount of attention to internal stimuli that is associated with past events and interpreting the world from that point of view. The ability to process multiple stimuli simultaneously becomes diminished, and perception narrows. Any sensation similar to the trauma leads to the perception that one is in danger.

The problem with becoming hyper-vigilant in an effort to foresee danger is that one becomes less and less able to identify it. Breathing patterns linked to activated states occur whenever there is the implicit memory or activating trigger. At that point, recognition of safety also becomes impossible. Danger is everywhere, fear is constant. That aroused breath cycle is a reminder and "proof" to the body that danger is real.

In trauma therapy, we practice interrupting and resourcing these moments, teaching the body to recognize itself and interrupt the dysfunctional breathing pattern.

Five-Step Resourcing

PURPOSE

The goal of this exercise is to stabilize and re-direct the client into a somatic resourcing.

INSTRUCTIONS

Overview of the five steps:

1. Assess for what kind of resource is available. Ask the client what they consider resourceful. When possible, ask if they can sense a physical resource in the body (e.g., feeling the feet on the ground). Discuss and develop with the client.

2. Name the experience of this resource.

3. Shift the client into mindful awareness.

4. Reference and immerse the client in the present-moment experience.

5. Study the experience of the resource. Follow up by asking the client to study the details of their experience. You want to watch for positive outcomes and possible new insights.

Concrete example questions/statements to facilitate the five steps:

Step 1 - Assess and identify the resource

Assess what kind of somatic resource is available.

- "What kind of resource do you find helpful?"
- "Is this a physical experience?"
- "What do you consider safe, pleasurable, or calming in this moment?"
- "Is there an image, a sensation, or a feeling in your body that you can reference right now?"
- "Describe a moment of resource."
- "Where does this resource live in your body right now?"

Step 2 - Name the experience of resource

Preferential contact of resource: Help unfold the "goodness" of the experience.

- "There seems to be this calm feeling in your…."
- "When you think of your 'X,' you relax right away."
- "As you sense into your feet you seem to…."
- "It seems that this reminds you of something pleasant."

Step 3 - Shift client into mindful awareness

It's important to ask the client to slow down.

- "Go ahead and focus on this resource."
- "Slow down and see if you can be with this resource."
- "Take your time noticing that the resource is here as well."
- "Just let yourself notice how, what, where.... the resource shows up right now."

Step 4 - Reference and immerse in the present-moment experience

Ask the client to dwell in the experience. It is by staying with the present-moment experience that the body will respond.

- "Notice what gets in the way of being with this resource right now."
- "Stay with this resource."
- "Notice how the activation shows up and choose the resource."
- "Go ahead and let yourself be with the resource."
- "It's okay to stay with that one resource."
- "Let yourself trust the resource."
- "Keep choosing the resource."

Step 5 - Study the experience of resource

Study the experience and watch for negative beliefs or attempts to undermine the resource. Ask them to stay with the resource if possible.

- "Go ahead and see if you can develop this resource."
- "Can you just let this be here right now?"
- "Study the quality and details of this resource right now."
- "Get curious about how this resource informs you."
- "How do you notice this resource impacting you right now?"
- "Discover what wants to happen."
- "See if you can stay with and study the resource and notice what the activation does right now."

client exercise

Dual Awareness Practice

PURPOSE

By cultivating dual awareness, you are able to process old trauma "one arousal cycle at a time." Each time an arousal cycle is successfully processed, it signals the body of a successful completion of the trauma responses and embeds resources. This exercise will slow down that cycle and establish a new breathing and body pattern.

INSTRUCTIONS

- Have the client imagine an event where arousal reaches within the window of tolerance and towards the upper regions. Make sure this is not high-arousal activation; you want to be able to work with your experience and not be overwhelmed.
- Now instruct the client "drop the content" and practice dual awareness. This means not thinking about the story, but focusing on the somatic awareness.
- Use general somatic accessing questions/statements.

Ask for details of the somatic experience:

- "Allow yourself to witness your experience **AS** you are having it."
- "Where does that sensation begin and end?"

Breath focus:

- "What does the breath do?"
- "Notice how your breath is doing…" (Describe to the client what you track, especially the location of the breath.)
- "How do you want to be breathing?"

Moving memory:

- "Keep moving through time. What happens next?"
- Stay with just the experience of that sensation: "Take plenty of time to just feel that sensation, the breath…"
- "Allow the image/memory to be part of it, but not rule you right now. Come back to the sensations, the quality of the breath."

Movement and responses:

- Work with spontaneous, involuntary sensate responses: "As much as you're comfortable, just allow your spine to vibrate."
- "Notice how your body responds right now. It's okay to follow the impulses."

Harvest - Regulation:

- Savor: "Savor the sensation of your energy moving."
- "Notice how your breath is calming, regulating. Deepen that."
- "Stay with feeling the wave-like breath right now."
- "Allow for your body to be this calm…."

client
exercise

Flat Back Strength

PURPOSE

This strength-building exercise will engage your legs and the core of your body. This exercise can be integrated into a session when the body needs a defined boundary or the client needs to feel strength in their core.

INSTRUCTIONS

Before: On a scale 1-10, I feel grounded: _____

- Start standing and lean against the wall with a flat back.
- Feel your feet on the ground.
- Slowly slide your back down along the wall.
- Press into the wall and "sit down," having knees at a 90-degree angle. Make sure you don't strain your knees.
- Engage your core muscles and your legs. The weight should be carried by the large muscle groups of the upper leg.
- Relax the rest of your body; no tension in the neck. Have your eyes be softly focused.
- Sit here until you feel a small vibration moving through the leg muscles.
- Then slowly straighten your spine by sliding along the wall towards standing.
- Lean and rest for a moment. Then push off the wall to stand.
- Notice the connection with the ground.
- You can repeat this two to three times, but make sure you don't overtire the legs. This is meant to be enlivening, not to tire and push the body.

After: On a scale 1-10, I feel grounded: _____

Reflection:

I notice my legs being: _____

My core is: _____

My overall energy is: _____

I feel my boundaries as: _____

client
worksheet

Embodied Self-Awareness
and Resourcing

PURPOSE

This tool helps you start building your own repertoire of what works for you. Resource tools are an invitation to take charge of what helps you best. This chart helps you reflect on your challenges and your particular remedies. Think about your qualities and traits and what you can do to train towards embodiment.

INSTRUCTIONS

Using the chart on page 243, reflect on your traits and challenges. What practices can help you deepen the qualities of reliance and growth? What works?

Traits and Challenges

Challenge	Qualities	Traits	What mindfulness or embodiment practice helps you here?	What do I need to practice more? How can I get support here?
The body carries tension, anxiety, depression	Curious about exploring embodiment and self-awareness	• Ability to feel and sense experience "as is" • Ability to be with emotional pain and not suppress • View of learning and growth		
Body memories; strong emotions	Trusting in the body's intelligence	• Ability to feel pleasure and tolerate positive emotions • Open to negative feelings and inquiring into origin of them • Basic trust in one's goodness • Perceiving the body as an ally		
Overwhelming emotions; complicated relationship stories; no easy solutions	Tolerating grey zones of experiences and relationships	• Able to ask for help • Thinking clearly and accessing body sensations as self-awareness • Ability to feel self-compassion and kindness • Able to make choices that are supportive		
Challenging life phases, crises, stuck places; faced with obstacles	Open to "being" aspect of experience in the flow of process	• Ability to see one's emotional life as transitory • Ability to put challenge into perspective • Able to forgive self and others • Ability to see a spiritual or growth aspect of life's challenges • Seeing self as an unfolding process		

Name Your Resource

PURPOSE

Resources are both internal and external. They stabilize us and help us navigate life at different times. Think of the various kinds of resources you have in your life. These can range from family connections to your favorite activity, your pet, causes you care about, or spiritual practices. Think of what makes you happy, resourced, and grounded so that you can effectively deal with life's challenges.

INSTRUCTIONS

Take an inventory of the resources you have in your life.

External Resources	Relationship Resources	Internal Resources

SOMATIC COHERENCE

Coherence is the absence of stress and trauma; the inner and outer sense of well-being are aligned. When trauma happens, it happens to the body and the person. The biological responses to stress and trauma strive towards emotional and physical well-being. These inherent healing mechanisms are helped by learning how to tune to the needs of the body and learning how we heal.

Somatic coherence refers to the feelings and sensations in the body as a state of being. When the stressors subside we are restored; we feel coherent again—mental functioning returns, emotional upheaval calms, and physical pain subsides. Being connected with one's own inner balance and well-being is crucial to the healing process. Somatic coherence is how the body, mind and heart align again after being dysregulated. Learn how to read and cultivate your own coherence with these somatic practices.

You want to understand what your optimum health and well-being is. Knowing your inner coherence is an emotional baseline so you can notice right away when you are feeling stressed and make shifts before stress builds up and creates incoherence. Learning how to tend to your inner coherence is essential to deal with stressors of daily life. When you master somatic coherence, you can deal with one stressor at the time and avoid burn-out. By tuning to your body, befriending the small stressors and paying attention to your breath, the resulting body wellness will make a big difference in the longevity of your health.

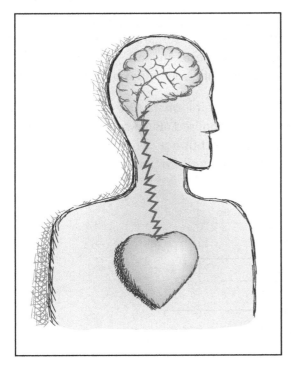

INCOHERENCE

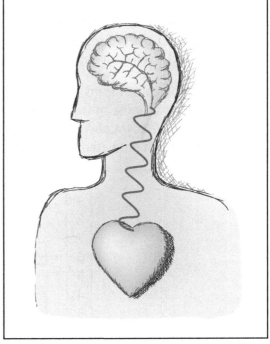

COHERENCE

client worksheet

Reflect on Your Own
Somatic Coherence

PURPOSE

Learn to rate yourself what you mean by somatic coherence. Somatic coherence is how you feel at your best and when most in tune with your body, heart and mind. How do you know when you are feeling emotionally aligned with your intentions? What are the tell-tale signs you know when you feel at your best?

This tool helps you rate yourself on what you consider High, Balanced or Low Somatic Coherence.

INSTRUCTIONS

Identify what helps you get there and what gets in the way. What derails you from feeling well and coherent? Spend some time reflecting on the inner derailers, such as negative self-talk or triggers that interfere with your somatic coherence. Derailers are internal negative voices that will impact your self-esteem and your body confidence. These can be voices of doubt, worry or anxiety that stifle your curiosity and creativity.

"High Coherence" means you are feeling energetic—full of creative potential, energy and the ability to handle stressors without being compromised. "Balanced" is being in harmony with yourself. "Low Coherence" is being able to cope, but not performing at your best. This is a self-assessment based on what you know about your own body.

```
10
 9    ┌─────────────────────┐
 8    │  High Coherence     │
 7    └─────────────────────┘
 6    ┌─────────────────────┐
 5    │  Balanced           │
 4    └─────────────────────┘
 3    ┌─────────────────────────┐
 2    │  Low Coherence          │
 1    └─────────────────────────┘
```

Part 1

High Somatic Coherence for me means I am_____

Balanced Somatic Coherence for me means I am_____

Low Somatic Coherence for me means I am_____

What restores my somatic coherence? _____

Reflection:

Take a moment and reflect on what stands in the way of your optimum somatic coherence? What internal negative voice? What are the worries or anxieties that hold you back?

My inner derailers are:

_____

_____

_____

_____

My inner derailers need:

_____

_____

_____

_____

Part 2

Rate yourself on the Somatic Coherence Scale. If you are on the High Coherence level, take a moment and read over what derails you. How can you relate to your derailers when you are in High Somatic Coherence? Compare this to a time when you are in Low Somatic Coherence and your relationship with your inner derailers at that time. Any differences?

Write to your inner derailers when you are in High Somatic Coherence:

I understand that:

_____

_____

I like you to know:

_____

_____

_____

Next time when I am in Low Coherence, I want you to help me to do:

_____

_____

_____

therapist
worksheet

Tracking Your Client from Body Activation to Somatic Coherence

PURPOSE

This tool will help you track what body-wisdom tools work for your client. Start tracking the key areas such as breath, attention, eye movement, posture, body movement, and ability to be mindful. By charting these body cues, you will gain a more comprehensive understanding of what somatic cues belong to the trauma and stress assessment. This tool should be used in addition to any other clinical assessment tools you are using. Although it can be confusing and difficult to track the body and what it means, this chart will help you to keep noticing and inquiring.

In addition, look for somatic coherence. Learn to understand when your client is in balance and what that feels and looks like for them. Each client will have a different baseline of what they consider "coherent;" therefore, it's important to notice what your client considers to be "somatic coherence" so you can learn and understand their internal experience.

INSTRUCTIONS

The following chart lists key areas of the body to track for activation. This can include what you track in any given session and what is self-reported. This chart can be used to help you track a client's body patterns and behaviors over time, in order to aid how you use the somatic tools in this book. Track the tools you are using and what does and doesn't work. This will help you make sure you are being most effective. Please use your professional discretion and training to make the right interventions.

Somatic Cues	Notes/Observations	Body Wisdom Tools	Worked Well	Needs Adjusting	Somatic Coherence Cues
Breath Region					
Upper Chest					
Mid-Chest					
Lower Chest					
Breath Quality					
Fast					
Rapid					
Held					
Frozen					
Fear/Anxiety mixed with breath					

Somatic Cues	Notes/Observations	Body Wisdom Tools	Worked Well	Needs Adjusting	Somatic Coherence Cues
Staccato					
Breath Awareness					
Able to focus on breath					
Easily distracted					
Avoids breath awareness					
Fearful of breath awareness					
Attention					
Able to focus					
Over-focused, tunnel vision					
Distracted, with anxiety					
Distracted, with anger					
Distracted, with somatic complaints					
Easily interrupted and distracted					
Eyes					
Scanning, with vigilance					
Scanning, with fear/terror					
Side glancing					
Vacant stare: under-focused					
Intent stare: over-focused					
Posture					
Stiff and held					
Upright, non-moving					
Tight muscles					
Braced posture					

Somatic Cues	Notes/Observations	Body Wisdom Tools	Worked Well	Needs Adjusting	Somatic Coherence Cues
Slacked posture					
Movement					
Twitching, legs					
Twitching, arms					
Twitching, hands					
Shaking, spine					
Shaking, legs					
Shaking, arms/hands					
Shaking, whole body					
Repetitive movements (any part of the body)					
Hands, wringing/clutching					
Hands, sitting on/tucked under					
Feet, moving/shuffling					
Feet, stacked or tucked under					
Arms, crossed					
Mindful Capacity					
Can't become mindful at all					
Jumps out of mindfulness					
Racing mind/thoughts					
Spaces out					
Inner world absorbed					
Experiences inner world as threat					
Other Body Cues					

CHAPTER 24
Shame and Trauma

"Shame is an acutely self-conscious state in which the self is "split," imagining the self in the eyes of the other; by contrast, in guilt the self is unified. In shame, the self is passive; in guilt the self is active. Shame is an acutely painful and disorganizing emotion; guilt may be experienced without intense affect. Shame engenders a desire to hide, escape, or to lash out at the person in whose eyes one feels ashamed. By contrast, guilt engenders a desire to undo the offense, to make amends. Finally, shame is discharged in restored eye contact and shared, good-humored laughter, while guilt is discharged in an act of reparation."

- Judith Lewis Herman

Feelings of shame can arise when working with the body in general. Deep-seated beliefs about the body can surface and the client might experience feelings that are "dark and shameful." From a somatic psychotherapy perspective, these are important moments not to be missed. You can gently acknowledge and normalize this in your client with empathic statements. Shame feelings want to hide again and the tendency is to want to hide along with the client as these moments are truly difficult to witness. The very fact that you can accept these vulnerable moments is healing.

Shame feelings often surface particularly when trauma is associated. There can be a range of emotions connected along with it such as:

- A strong urge to hide and withdraw emotionally
- Negative self-criticism, bordering on abusive self-talk
- Feeling humiliated, ashamed
- The urge to be secretive and avoidant

SHAME AND SOMATIC INTERVENTIONS

The experience of shame with trauma clients can bring forth a high degree of body dissociation. Since shame is an involuntary response in the body, similar to the flee and freeze responses, the client can feel internally trapped. The social pressure to stay in the therapeutic relationship can trigger the client into feeling "wrong." Since they can't leave the office in that moment (and some might), they may experience feeling stuck. This can heighten previous trauma, or reinforce the internal messages that come along with it. Shame never feels good and most of us want to get away from it or hide the experience as quickly as possible. Shame can bring forth a tendency to want to be secretive and hide the true self.

As therapists, we are also somatically inclined to want to help cover up that moment of shame and collude in looking away or not mentioning what is happening. We know instinctively that we don't want to say something to make it worse, and yet not saying anything is also a bad option. When working somatically, you want to encourage kindness and a gentle, mindful exploration of the shame feelings. At the same time, you want to give room for the client to retreat and move on.

In the beginning, exploring shame can be after the fact, meaning that once the shame attack passes, you can invite the client to reflect and be mindful of the past experience. The more you talk about it and work with it, the less power the shame will have. You are normalizing this body feeling like any other feeling in the body. Gentle inquiry questions such as, "That was powerful. Is there anything that makes you curious about what just happened?" can be enough to have the client gain some control and interest in the experience.

Once the client has embraced this, you have an opportunity to work with the shame attack when it happens. The truth is that the actual shame attack lasts only seconds; however, the internal experience and the meaning it holds can last a lifetime. The less power these lifelong messages have, the less frequently the shame attacks occur.

Often past shame experiences are coupled with having been "outed" by someone. The classic example of turning red and then being called out for being red-faced hints at the dark power of being outed. The body responds to being an outcast as a life threat. Being cast out from our human tribe is a hardwired primal fear and can mean life or death. The body registers this and responds with the flight, fight, freeze system.

VERBAL CUES

If the client uses the following words to describe their experience, pay attention to any corresponding body cues that may indicate shame is present: *"Ridiculous, foolish, stupid, dumb, humiliated, helpless, inept, dependent, small, inferior, embarrassed, worthless, weak, idiotic."*

BREATHING CUES

When a client talks about the shame experience or has a shame attack, pay close attention to breath quality. You will see breath patterns similar to when the client has a trauma activation. Breath is one of the easiest body cues to track for the presence of shame. Look for cues such as: Flat and held breath, constriction in the throat, difficulty breathing, small and measured breaths as if sipping the breath in, complaints of chest constriction, tight lips and short bursts of breath in or out, or rapid breath high in the chest.

Intervention Sequence with Shame

PURPOSE

These shame intervention steps are gentle ways to help the client befriend the shame experience and learn to master it rather than withdraw from it. Since the client feels somatically taken hostage by the intensity of the shame, you need to take the lead in helping them through this moment. Make sure you are kind and accepting of the experience. It is easy to get triggered as the therapist; be kind and clear. Each time you do this successfully, you are re-training the brain and body into new possibilities.

INSTRUCTIONS

- **Name and befriend:** Very kindly acknowledge the shame state: *"I am noticing that there are a lot of feelings and sensations right now. Seems they are all talking at once. I understand how intense that is for you…"*

- **Take the lead:** The client is stuck in their shame and wants to hide. As the therapist, you must take a gentle lead: *"Let's try shifting you a little bit. Can you focus on your lower belly right now and take some slow breaths? I know that might feel a little clumsy to you right now—that's okay. I can do it with you."* You can also offer body resources you know the client will accept, such as feet, legs—places in the body you know are safe or grounding.

- **Guide them out and normalize:** Mindfulness is barely possible, thinking is out, so you need to take them out of the experience by guiding them to their resourced self: *"There is a lot of heat in your hands, right? That's okay. Just let that be there; it will pass." "You can watch these sensations pass. Let me help you do that…"*

- **Track the body:** Once you see parasympathetic release and more eye contact, you can name what this was: *"You had some shame come up, huh?" "Yes, it seemed a little self-conscious there for you."*

- **Psycho-educate and have them integrate with resource:** *"What did that remind you of? Now that you are not so activated, let's talk about what that was." "You know that's what happens when our bodies get scared, we feel shame. It's a very normal response."* Contextualize the shame experience into the normal range of a trauma response. For example: *"Shame is a healthy response and reminds us that we are moral beings. We feel and sense what is not right." "When you felt shame as a little girl when 'X' happened, you knew that was wrong, huh?"*

Outing the Shame Monster

PURPOSE

Shame is an involuntary response. By "outing" the shame and making it conscious, it will lose its power and secrecy. This exercise is designed to help you become comfortable with your shame monsters and make them less powerful. It's important to stay mindful and slow with this exercise.

INSTRUCTIONS

Complete the following statements/questions.

1. *"I remember being ashamed of…"* Study the response in your body first! Then write down the first thing that comes to your mind.

_____

2. *"I remember my body feeling the shame. It felt like…"*

_____

3. *"I now remember the shame of the past, and I feel…"*

_____

4. *"My 'shame name' for this monster is…"*

_____

5. If you could draw this shame monster, what would it look like? Draw it now on a separate piece of paper.

6. Come back to your body now; breathe and feel. What do you notice in this moment?

therapist worksheet

Identifying and Reframing Shame Attacks

PURPOSE

Shame is a natural response of the body. But it is also an involuntary response that can cause secondary stress as it can feel intense sudden and overwhelming. Shame can arise when we engage with a behavior that is morally, ethically or cultural incongruent. You can feel a sense of failure to protect yourself or being conflicted inside. Shame can also arise by being a witness or bystander to an act of violation that is beyond one's control and forces to witness. Or a behavior one is engaged in without consciousness at the time and soon reflection brings feelings of shame. Shame is a response of the body, that comes and goes like a flash. Yet the effect of shame can linger and secondary responses can arise such as wanting to cover up the feelings, being defensive, aggression toward the person that notices or wanting to retreat emotionally and physically.

As a therapist working with shame you need to be sensitive and considerate of the person's experience. The pull towards wanting to cover up the shame moment is great. It does not feel comfortable in the present moment. Knowing that the moment will pass is crucial, because then you can work with the shame moment and help the client out of the stuck place. Shame reinforces shame over time if it's not understood or worked with.

Part one is for the therapist to work with shame themselves when they notice they got stuck or triggered in their own shame. Part two you can use with your client when the shame has just happened. There is an ideal window once the shame has dissipated a little bit that you might find a receptivity to work with the shame directly. If the shame is too far in memory it's not alive enough for the client. If you address it right away while it's happening you might further activate the shame. Being ashamed of the shame is a common experience. Make sure you are well resourced as the therapist and be VERY kind with your client. You want to see the "goodness" of shame and not add to the shame experience.

Shame is a fleeting moment but an important one. So you want to have the courage to work with it. It is easy to let that moment pass, but I encourage you to work with it. Shame wants to be known, there is a deeper meaning underneath. If you are kind, open and receptive and truly stay with the client's body experience you will see that a whole new possibility can open up. The client might be able to learn what has gotten them ashamed in the first place. Shame is like an inner moral compass that wants to be known. Don't be thrown off by the strong somatic manifestation. Remember it is a fleeting moment, it won't last.

Important Tip:
Avoid calling it "shame" in the moment of a shame attack. Try naming it by describing it in a round-about way and wait for the client to name it shame. This is an important self-empowering step! Here some ways to name the intensity of the shame attack:

"I see you having a strong response."
"Looks like this is tough for you right there, huh?"
"Your body is responding right now, what are you aware off?"
"Seems it's hard to put into words what your body is expressing."
"Not easy to grasp what is happening right now."
"Notice how your body is responding and see if you can get curious about what this is."
"Lot's of conflicting emotions and sensations right there."

INSTRUCTIONS

Know your own shame responses. Do your own shame homework. Inquire into the following questions. Especially when you are noticing being triggered by a client who has a shame response.

Self-reflection questions:

• What happened to you when your client got shame activated?

_____

• Tune into the moment of the shame attack and somatically tune into your body of what that felt like. Note the body cues and your thoughts.

_____

• Where in your body do you notice shame? Any familiar places?

_____

• Note the body cues that indicate a shame attack next time and reframe it into a personal alarm system. The alarm is a supposed to help you redirect this moment into a positive action towards resourcing yourself. My body's shame alarm is:

_____

• Now list and note the places in the body that can help you next time when this happens. My body resources are:

_____

• List one positive rename of shame for yourself. What if shame had a positive message for you? What would it say?

_____

Reflection:

How does shame make me small? _____

client
worksheet

Identifying Shame Attacks and Preventing Shame Spirals

Part 2

INSTRUCTIONS

Work with the client on their shame attack and how to prevent a negative emotional spiral. Remember, ideally the intensity of the shame attack has passed, the client has named it as shame, or you are exploring what this strong response is right after.

Step 1 - Identify

1. Make a kind observation
   - *"That was an intense response, huh?"*

2. Invite curiosity and non-judgment
   - *"Care to get curious about what just happened?"*

3. Explore the body response without any charge
   - *"Let's stay with what you are noticing right now in your body. Explore a little what this is like."*

4. Name, reflect and contextualize the experience
   - *"See if you can label this place in your body, or name this experience you just had. What would you call this?"*

Step 2 - Name and reflect

Now that you have more information. See if you can label and name this experience.

_____

_____

Make a very quick drawing or name this. Don't think, but rather trust your first response.

First response drawing:

Look at the name for drawing and reflect on this right now.

What does it sound or look like?

What is familiar?

When does this shame attack happen?

What are some of the triggers you know?

_____

_____

_____

_____

Step 3-Reframe the Shame Attack

Take one aspect of this shame attack drawing, naming or reflection that stands out to you. For example you can take a word and then work on the next step with just that word. If you had a word like "hide," then you would ask: What does "hide" have to teach me? If "hide" has a message what would it say? If "hide" was brilliant and intelligent what would "hide" mean?

What does _____have to teach me?

If _____had a message what would it say?

If _____was brilliant and intelligent what would

_____mean?

Now make a new statement of the shame attack with this information you just discovered.

My shame attack in the moment means that I am…

_____

_____

_____

Any other insights?

_____

client
worksheet

Sun Rays into Your Body

PURPOSE

This exercise is the counterweight to the shame experience. Shame makes the body feel small and contracted. To "thaw" the body open, you can invite the body back in a gentle and progressive way. Visualize the sun's rays meeting your belly and warming you up gradually.

INSTRUCTIONS

- Imagine a safe space in nature. Perhaps you are laying on a smooth rock, the earth or a cozy bench.

- Place your hand on your belly button.

- Imagine that the sun is just right: Warming, bright and inviting.

- Begin to breathe slowly into the belly button area underneath your hand.

- Now imagine the warm sun radiating into that belly button and warming you up. Can you feel the sun's rays in your body? Concentrate on the image.

- What happens when you feel the warmth? See if you can go with the sensations in the body and savor them; see what comes up. Track your body and breath. Does the breath slow down? What becomes available as you do this?

- Observe the shifting and how your body returns to the calm state.

- Notice how the bright glare of the shame has been replaced with the warm glow of the sun.

Reflection:

- How does shame make me small? _____

_____

_____

- What triggers my shame attack?_____
_____
_____

- What is helpful when I am in it?_____
_____
_____

- What resources within me counteract the shame?_____
_____
_____

- What do I need to remind myself of afterwards? _____
_____
_____

Bibliography

Baka, D. (1999). *Minding the Body: Clinical Uses of Somatic Awareness,* (pp. 4-5). Guilford Press: New York.

Bainbridge Cohen, B. (1993). *Sensing, Feeling and Action: The Experiential Anatomy of Body-Mind Centering.* Contact Editions: Northampton, MA.

Domasio, A. (2000). *The Feeling of What Happens: Body and Emotion in the Making of Consciousness.* Harcourt San Diego, CA

Field, T. (2003). *Touch.* The MIT Press: London, England.

Field, T. (2014). *Touch. A Bradford Book.* The MIT Press: Cambridge, MA.

Fogel, A. (2009). *Body Sense: The Science and Practice of Embodied Self-Awareness.* W.W. Norton: New York.

Franklin, E. (2012). *Dynamic Alignment Through Imagery.* 2nd ed. Human Kinetics. Champaign, IL.

Hartley, L. (1995). *Wisdom of the Body Moving: An Introduction to Body-Mind Centering.* North Atlantic Books: Berkeley, CA.

Heller, L. (2012). *Healing Developmental Trauma: How Early Trauma Affects Self-Regulation, Self-Image, and the Capacity for Relationship.* North Atlantic Books: Berkeley, CA.

Johnson, D. (1983). Body. Beacon Press, Boston,MA.

Levine, P. (2010). *In an Unspoken Voice: How the Body Releases Trauma and Restores Goodness.* North Atlantic Books: Berkeley, CA.

McHose, C. (2006). *How Life Moves: Explorations in Meaning and Body Awareness.* North Atlantic Books: Berkeley, CA.

Mischke-Reeds, M. (2015). *8 Keys to Practicing Mindfulness: Practical Strategies for Emotional Health and Well-Being.* W.W. Norton: New York.

Olsen, A. (1991). *Body Stories: A Guide to Experiential Anatomy.* Station Hill Press: New York.

Prendergast, J. (2015). *In Touch: How to Tune in to the Inner Guidance of Your Body and Trust Yourself.* Sounds True: Boulder, CO.

Ray, R. (2008). *Touching Enlightenment: Finding Realization in the Body.* Sounds True: Boulder, CO.

Weiss, H., Johanson, G., & Monda, L. (2015). *Hakomi Mindfulness-Centered Somatic Psychotherapy: A Comprehensive Guide to Theory and Practice.* W.W. Norton: New York.

Made in the USA
Monee, IL
04 January 2021